James Laurence Laughlin

Gold and prices since 1873

James Laurence Laughlin

Gold and prices since 1873

ISBN/EAN: 9783744739597

Printed in Europe, USA, Canada, Australia, Japan

Cover: Foto ©ninafisch / pixelio.de

More available books at **www.hansebooks.com**

GOLD AND PRICES

1873

BY

J. LAURENCE LAUGHLIN

HEAD PROFESSOR OF POLITICAL ECONOMY IN THE UNIVERSITY
OF CHICAGO

Reprinted from QUARTERLY JOURNAL OF ECONOMICS, *April, 1887*

The University of Chicago Press

1895

New York
State College of Agriculture
At Cornell University
Ithaca, N. Y.

Library

CHAPTER I.

GOLD AND PRICES SINCE 1873.

§ I. MUCH of the difference of opinion as to the significance of recent movements of prices is due to the fact that the value of gold is a ratio which varies with a variation in either of its terms. Whether commodities fall in relation to gold or gold rises in relation to commodities, in either case the value of gold has risen. The same phenomena, therefore, may be due to radically different causes. So that, admitting the fall of prices, it is said, on the one hand, that the rise in the value of gold is due to some cause affecting gold itself, such as scarcity; and, on the other hand, it is claimed that the fall in prices is due to causes connected solely with commodities, and not with gold.

The believers in the scarcity value of gold substantiate their position by reference to the falling off in the annual production of gold; the unusual demands for gold since 1873, by Germany, Italy, and the United States; stringencies in the money market; the increased use of gold in the arts; the claim that the fall of prices is general; the exceptional character of the depression of trade since 1873; the general existence of low wages, profits, and rents; and the absence of any progress since 1873 in the means of economizing gold and silver. These opinions have been prominently associated with Mr. Robert Giffen,* the statistician of the English Board of Trade, and Mr. Goschen,† the present Chancellor of the Ex-

---

* *Journal of the Statistical Society* (London), March, 1879.

† *Journal of the Institute of Bankers*, April 18, 1883.

chequer; while the evident connection of the main proposition with bimetallism has given it a semi-political character, and many supporters in both Europe and America.

§ II. Inasmuch as the rise in the value of gold since 1873 is in proportion to the fall of prices, it is a matter of some importance to look critically at the facts in regard to prices. With this object in view, the more important tables of prices since 1850 have been collected in the Appendix, with explanations as to the methods of computation, sources, and reliability. It is hoped that a comparison of the diverse methods and results of these tables will serve a useful purpose.

Hitherto, the figures of the London *Economist* for twenty-two articles have been almost universally used as evidence in regard to the movement of prices; but it is time that the worship of this fetich should cease.* Of late, much more trustworthy tables have been published.

In Chart I., a comparison is presented of the prices in Great Britain, Germany, France, and the United States. The untrustworthiness of the *Economist* table as a basis for inferences in regard to causes affecting the whole world will be seen at a glance in the years 1862–67. The table of Mr. Sauerbeck,† however, which gives the prices of thirty-eight articles, but all of raw produce, furnishes a somewhat better view of the movement of English prices to the present day. The French prices ‡ show a less rise to 1873 and a less fall since 1873 than the English figures, which accords with what we know as to the exemption of France from the violence of the crisis of 1873. The table of American prices cannot be depended upon. It is in-

---

* For detailed criticism, see Appendix, Table A.

† For the relative value of these tables, see the notes in the Appendix.

‡ The number 100 in this table corresponds on the chart to 123.6 of Soetbeer's table, which is the average of the latter's numbers for 1865–69 (the years used as a basis in the French prices).

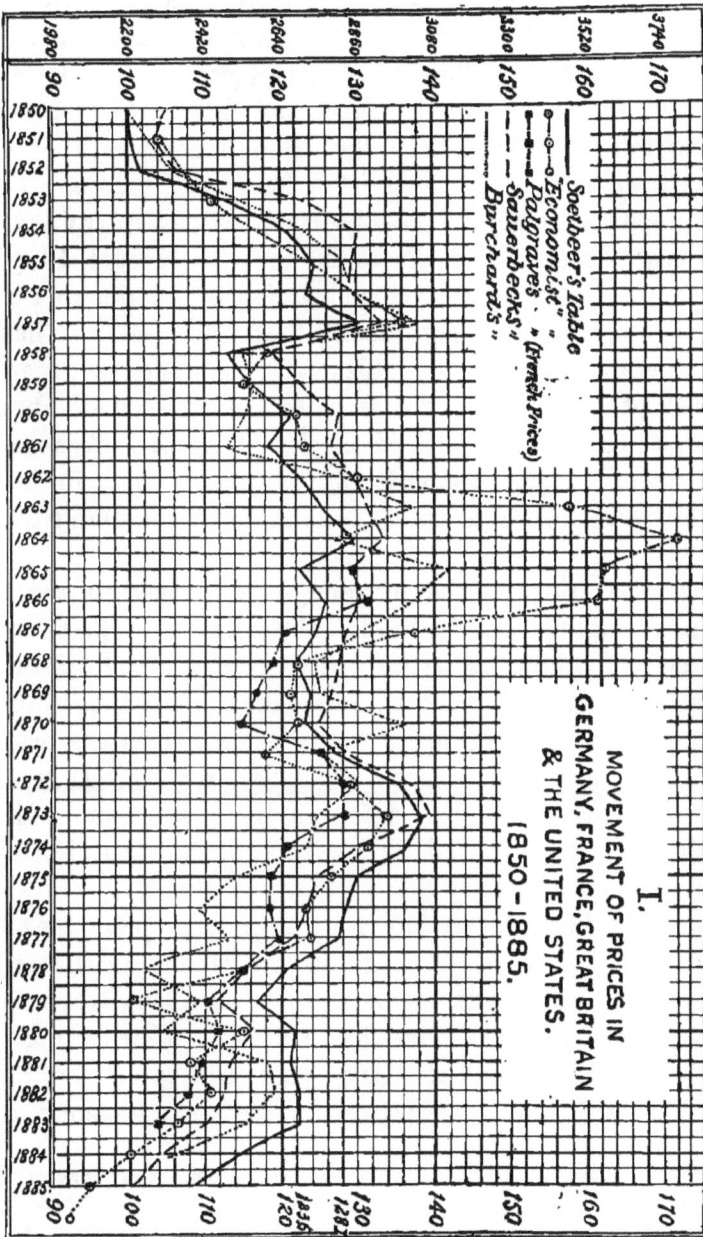

I.

MOVEMENT OF PRICES IN GERMANY, FRANCE, GREAT BRITAIN & THE UNITED STATES. 1850-1885.

Soetbeer's Table
"Economist"
Palgrave's (French Prices)
Sauerbeck's
Burchard's

serted only for the sake of comparison. The Hamburg
prices, published by Dr. Soetbeer, in the second edition of
his *Materialien* (1886), furnish the most satisfactory, accurate, and complete collection of prices yet made. It will
be seen that, while Sauerbeck's English figures * show a
greater fall since 1873 than the Hamburg prices, they do
not fall so low in 1885 as the *Economist* prices. The
very important fact to be observed, however, from the
Hamburg table is that prices in 1885 were still 10 per
cent. higher than they were before the discoveries of gold
(1847–50) ; and it is significant that prices seem to have
fallen less as we go to tables which include a greater
number of articles. There is thus a difference of about
30 per cent. in the results of the Hamburg and *Economist*
table, much to the discredit of the latter ; and, in fact,
the *Economist* table is not of a kind to be compared with
the other.

The separation of the movements of prices in special
groups of commodities in the Hamburg tables, as presented
in Chart II., shows a striking divergence in the prices of
agricultural, animal, mineral, and manufactured products.
The eye is at once struck with the great rise in the prices
of animal and agricultural products since 1850; while
there has been the expected fall in the case of manufactured goods, accompanied by a surprising fall in the prices
of mineral products.

Among other illustrations † of economic principles to
be seen in these charts, there is one which Englishmen
may well consider. It seems possible that English prices
have fallen since 1873 more than prices in other countries.
If so, may this not be attributed to a readjustment of the
equation of Internation Demand, due to a lessened de-

---

* The standard 100 in Sauerbeck's table represents the average of the
years 1866–77, which corresponds on the chart to 128.7 of Soetbeer's table.

† A verification is given of the principles laid down by Mr. Cairnes, *Leading Principles*, pp. 117–46, on derivative laws of value.

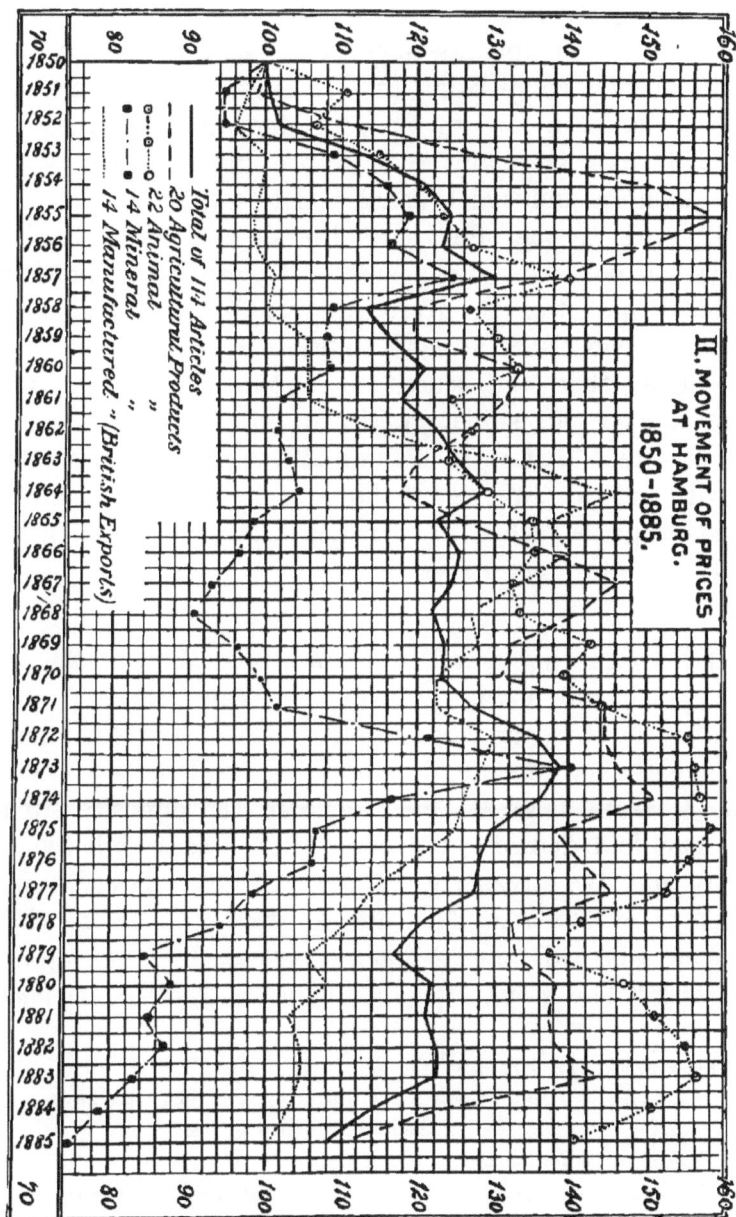

II. MOVEMENT OF PRICES AT HAMBURG. 1850-1885.

Total of 114 Articles
20 Agricultural Products
22 Animal "
14 Mineral "
14 Manufactured " (British Exports)

mand in other countries for England's products compared with England's demand for the products of other countries? Many complaints have been heard in England of the increasing competition of Germany, France, and the United States in foreign markets; for only since the war of 1870 have Germany and France given full play to their modern industrial spirit.* In fact, evidences are multiplying to the effect that the demand for English goods has not grown in a sufficiently gratifying manner. If this explanation be given full weight, it may suggest that other causes are at work to bring about a fall of English prices than the scarcity of gold. Too often, the reasoning on this subject takes for granted that what is true of Great Britain is true of all the rest of the world. It will not by any means be admitted that the lower range of prices, when once reached, has prevented prosperity † in other countries.

§ III. Granting a fall in prices since 1873 of 20 per cent., yet it will not be possible to reason directly from a fall of prices to a scarcity of gold. But this is the import of Laveleye's argument ‡ in answering Mulhall,— who had gone to quite as great an extreme in the opposite direction, and had denied § any connection whatever between prices and the quantity of the precious metals,— for Laveleye even classes Mill among the believers in what the Germans call the *Quantitäts-theorie*, by quoting his words: ‖ " The value of money depends, *caeteris paribus*,

---

* Cf. Fowler, *Appreciation of Gold*, p. 34.

† The clearings in the United States for October 1, 1886, were one-fourth larger than for October 1, 1885, at the lower range of prices.

‡ *Contemporary Review*, May, 1886, p. 632.

§ *History of Prices since the Year* 1850, pp. 138, 139; and *Contemporary Review*, August, 1885.

‖ Laveleye strangely omits the succeeding sentence: "In any state of things, however, except the simple and primitive one which we have supposed,

on its quantity, together with its rapidity of circulation.
. . . An increase of the quantity of money raises prices, and
a diminution lowers them. This is the most elementary
proposition in the theory of currency, and without it we
should have no key to any of the others." In his final
statement, however, Mill plainly says (B. III., chap. xi.,
§ 3), " In a state of commerce in which much credit is
habitually given, general prices at any moment depend
much more upon the state of credit than upon the quantity of money." The devices for economizing money
which the progress of society has developed render it impossible to say that prices depend directly upon the quantity of money.*

Credit in its full development is quite modern, and its
relation to prices is not always carefully defined. Mill,†
for example, prefaced his discussion of the effect of credit
on prices by the remark : " It is not, however, with ulti-
mate or average, but with immediate and temporary,
prices that we are now concerned." Now there is no
conceivable moment but that of a total stoppage of trade
when credit is not in active operation ; and as credit is

the proposition is only true, other things being the same ; and what those other
things are which must be the same we are not yet ready to pronounce " (B. III.,
chap. viii., § 4). In his final conclusion, quoted above by me, he pronounces
what they are.

* Frewen, *Nineteenth Century*, October, 1885, p. 595, carries the error still
further by claiming that prices change with the *production* of gold. One cannot assign much weight to Mr. Frewen, when he declares that capital is spent
rather than accumulated in the United States, because of the heavy taxation !
(p. 601). Dr. Soetbeer, *Materialien*, p. 81, reminds us that both Huskisson and
Jacob attributed the depression which prevailed in Europe after 1815 to a
scarcity of the precious metals. He also mentions an interesting book by
J. Helferich, published in 1843, which combated the *Quantitäts-theorie*, and
explained that credit can separate the function of a medium of exchange from
that of a measure of value, and can serve as the former without affecting the
latter. Most German bimetallists (excepting Dr. Arendt) agree with Messrs.
Giffen and Goschen in attributing the fall in prices and the depression of trade
to the scarcity of gold. But, on the other hand, Bourne, *Journal of Statistical
Society*, June, 1879, p. 417, who denies the scarcity of gold, claims, with Mulhall, that the quantity of gold has no relation to prices.

† B. III., chap. xii., § 1.

purchasing power of a highly efficient kind, often preferable to actual coin, it must be regarded as affecting prices not temporarily, but always, with greater or less force. At some periods it may be more actively used than at others.* In truth, in society as it exists to-day, the general level of prices for considerable periods (sufficiently long to permit the effect of changes in the business habits of the community, or changes in the existing stock of gold, to be felt) must depend upon a combination of the quantity of money with the various forms of credit. The two are inextricably bound together. So, therefore, the level of prices (so far as it is affected by the offer of purchasing power) depends on the expansion or contraction of two factors, quantity of money and credit, each of which may change to a considerable extent independently of each other. Both may increase or diminish together, or the gain of one may offset the loss of the other. A great collapse of credit, for example, without any change whatever in the quantity of the precious metals, might lower the general level of prices ; and, if this demoralization of confidence was sufficient to alter existing conditions of mind in the commercial classes, it would produce an effect over a considerable period of time. On the other hand, a period within which there occurred not only an enormous increase in the quantity of the metals used for money, but also an unusual expansion of credit, would show an advance of prices quite out of the natural order of things. Such a period was that from 1850 to 1873.

---

* Between 1833 and 1839 prices rose 22 1-2 per cent., and between 1839 and 1844 fell 44 per cent. ; and "this great oscillation," Jevons asserted, "was entirely due to the general expansion of trade and credit, and to its subsequent collapse." *Contemporary Review*, May, 1881, p. 752. Again, in 1857, at a time when the mines were yielding unprecedented quantities of gold, a collapse of credit produced a fall in prices of fully 15 per cent.

§ IV. The series of events which led to the expansion of trade and the collapse in 1873 were unprecedented in their magnitude. The greatest production from the mines which the world has ever seen was pouring gold into the channels of trade. In spite of the expansion of commerce and the absorption of gold by France, the new gold must have affected prices. But this set in motion other forces which had an effect on prices. The gold discoveries themselves created a spirit of adventure, and stimulated high hopes of gain in unusual ways. Then, too, a period of rising prices breeds speculation. The figures of home and foreign trade were swelled by the higher range of prices, and added to the buoyant feeling, under the inspiration of which new enterprises were eagerly entered upon. The Crimean War and the extraordinary rise of agricultural products (see Chart II.) aided the movement, which received but a partial check in the panic of 1857. The war in Italy of 1859 was followed by the Civil War in the United States in 1861. The latter produced a great rise in the prices of cotton, tobacco, and breadstuffs * in Europe ; and the issue of inconvertible paper drove gold out of the country. Then Italy also gave † up her specie after 1865. The war between Prussia and Austria added to the abnormal extension of trade, which in 1866 again received only a partial check. The years from 1867 to 1873, in the United States, witnessed an unlimited expansion of extravagance and overtrading, such as has been seldom equalled, accompanied by excessive railway building. Our imports were out of all proportion to our ability to pay for them.‡ In this period, also, came the Fran-

---

* This is seen in the *Economist* figures, in Chart I.

† The writer in the *Edinburgh Review* for July, 1886, p. 34, estimates the addition of gold to Europe from the United States and Italy as about $500,-000,000.

‡ Cf. Cairnes, *Leading Principles*, pp. 364–372.

co-German War of 1870, and the distribution of the indemnity of war by Germany. The extraordinary and exceptional demand for commodities in periods of war, at the very time of the great destruction of wealth, produced an unhealthy state of affairs; but on the outside all seemed fair, and men had begun to believe that prices were fated always to rise. The speculation in metals (see Chart II.) in 1873 was of an unparalleled kind.* Nothing, in fact, marks this period from 1850 to 1873 (as compared with the period from 1873 to 1886) more distinctly than the extreme variations in the rate of discount at the great banks of Europe. There were all the evidences of an unhealthy and abnormal condition of affairs. But the unchecked demand, when the actual power to buy had been greatly impaired, could not go on forever. When it was once found that men had been creating liabilities beyond their means to meet them, the end had come. The crisis of 1873 was the painful return to a consciousness of the real situation, after a prolonged fever of speculation for nearly twenty years, which had spread over many countries. The effects were the more serious because the disease had got such great headway. The period since 1873, on the other hand, is stamped by a radical change in methods of business; and a new epoch in production practically dates from that year. The peculiar changes in the organization of industry will themselves sufficiently explain any exceptional characteristics of the present period.

Those commodities, moreover, for which the demand in the period of overtrading had been most extended (and which were of a character capable of rapid production) would be the ones in regard to which, after the collapse, there would be the greatest difference between the power of production and the now lessened demand, based on normal wants. Demand and supply had been thrown out

* See Leroy-Beaulieu, *Revue des Deux Mondes*, May, 1886, p. 393.

of their reciprocal adjustment. Just as when a large building, erected by fitting one timber or board to another, is levelled to the ground by a tornado, exactly the same building can never again be reconstructed out of the old materials,— for reciprocal parts are wanting; — so, after a serious commercial disaster, like that of 1873, producers must make entirely new estimates as to the extent of demand, and supply must be adjusted to new conditions. In this way, a great derangement of trade and credit will produce unequal effects on different commodities.

§ V. To support the claim that we are now dealing with practically new conditions of production, no facts of the industrial situation since 1873 can be adduced which are more convincing than those relating to improvements and new sources of supply. The period following a great financial upheaval is naturally crowded with improvements in processes and in methods of lowering the cost of production. Necessity becomes the mother of invention. The extent to which producers have been driven by the fierce competition since 1873 to cheapen production leads to the inquiry how far the fall of prices can be accounted for by influences connected solely with commodities, and not with gold. If these influences have been widely extended, it will be strong evidence that the scarcity of gold has had less effect than some suppose.

In order to take a definite point of departure, I shall select from Mr. Goschen's list of articles * twenty-three which have fallen in price, and see whether the fall can be

---

* *Journal of Institute of Bankers*, May, 1883, pp. 277-279. These commodities, be it observed, are practically the same as those given by Mr. Giffen (see Appendix, Table E) to show the effects of a scarcity of gold in lowering prices. I have omitted from Mr. Goschen's table only cocoa, rice, indigo, cotton, hides, jute, and hewn timber; of which cocoa, cotton, and hides have practically not fallen at all; rice and jute are affected by the fall of silver; while indigo and timber are subject to peculiar fluctuations.

accounted for by conditions affecting each commodity itself : —

		1873.	1883.			1873.	1883.
		£ s. d.	£ s. d.			£ s. d.	£ s. d.
Sugar, brown,	cwt.	16 6	12 0	Wool, Australian,	lb.	2 0	1 10
" W. Indian	"	29 0	20 0	" alpaca,	"	2 9	1 3
Tea, Congou,	lb.	11½	5 0	Cochineal,	"	2 5	10
Coffee, Ceylon,	cwt.	87 0	70 0	Nitrate of soda,	cwt.	16 6	12 0
Wheat,	qr.	2 16 0	2 6 0	Saltpetre,	"	1 10 6	19 0
Pepper,	lb.	7	5½	Coals,	ton,	1 10 0	18 0
Iron, Scotch pig,	ton	6 7 0	2 9 0	Paper,		3 0 9	1 16 3
Lead, English,	"	21 10 0	13 15 0	Staves,	load,	10 0 0	5 0
Copper,	"	91 0 0	65 0 0	Mahogany,	"	11 12 0	9 5
Tin, foreign,	"	142 0 0	93 0 0	Railway carriages,		111 10 0	85 0
Wool, English,	lb.	2 3	10¾	Boots and shoes,	doz.	3 4 9	2 17 2
" Mohair,	"	3 3	1 8¼				

Taking these commodities in the order given, we find the fall in price of sugar due to the revolution in production since 1873 stimulated by the bounties on beet sugar in France, Germany, and Russia. The sugar of the West Indies was thus deprived of the vast European market. The supply was increased in this way without any connection whatever with the demand. From 1877 to 1882, the product of cane sugar increased 33 per cent., and that of beet sugar 40 per cent.*

Tea has fallen in price, owing to the great increase of production in Japan, which has risen to forty-five million pounds, to the enormous extension of tea cultivation in India, and to the addition of large supplies from Java and Ceylon ; while, unlike coffee, the consumption of tea has not increased in proportion to the increased production.†

* Leroy-Beaulieu, *Revue des Deux Mondes*, May, 1886, p. 398. According to Fowler, *Appreciation of Gold*, p. 23, the price of sugar in 1830 was £50 per ton; in 1840, £40 ; in 1880, £25 ; in 1886, £16. He finds, *Contemporary Review*, April, 1885, p. 539, the imports of unrefined sugar from Germany into England in 1884 were seven and three-fourths million hundred-weights as compared with four and one-half million hundred-weights in 1882.

† Tea is also bought with silver in the East, and, like jute, its gold price falls ; while the lowered freights have also had a serious influence. The exports of tea from India have quadrupled since 1873. See Sauerbeck, *ibid.*, p. 23.

Coffee has not fallen in price to the extent shown in Mr. Goschen's table. The average price at Hamburg in 1866–70 was expressed by 142; in 1876–80, by 207; and in 1881–85, by 139. Although the total production has increased,* the variations in the seasons cause violent fluctuations. The fall in the price of Brazilian coffee is accounted for by the extension of railways into the interior, which has dispensed with the carriage of coffee on mules to the seaports.

A fall in the prices of wheat and agricultural products seems to strengthen Mr. Goschen's argument, for commodities affected by the law of diminishing returns have a tendency to increase in price. A fall in the prices of such articles, therefore, might suggest a general cause, like the scarcity of gold. But at no time for centuries have there been in operation stronger forces to oppose this law than in recent years. The tremendous gains in cheaper transportation have, as never before, opened up new and superior wheat-growing soils,† so that the "margin of cultivation" for Europe is now found in India and the United States. The effect of this has been, irrespective of freight, to raise the margin of cultivation for Europe. It is only strange that the price of wheat has not fallen more seriously. Improved methods of farming, moreover, have enabled each acre to produce more than in 1870. Even in Europe, Leroy-Beaulieu thinks that, in the last twenty-five years, food has increased faster than population.

---

* Leroy-Beaulieu, *ibid.*, gives the production as follows: 1855, 321,000,000 tons; 1865, 422,000,000; 1875, 505,000,000; 1881, 588,000,000. The deliveries of Rio coffee in New York in 1873 were 68,863 tons, but in 1886 189,319 tons.

† The United States in 1870 had 83,000,000 acres planted with wheat, which was increased to 157,000,000 acres in 1884. India, moreover, increased her acreage from 18,000,000 in 1870 to 25,000,000 in 1884; while Europe planted 440,000,000 in 1870 and 482,000,000 in 1884. Leroy-Beaulieu, *ibid.*, p. 396. Neumann-Spallert, *Uebersichten der Weltwirthschaft*, p. 155, states that from 1869 to 1879 the production of cereals in Europe was actually doubled; while the imports of grain in 1869–70 were valued at $409,000,000, and in 1879 at $817,000,000.

Pepper has not fallen, but risen, in price since 1873.* For 1871–75 the average prices at Hamburg are expressed by 229.7, but for 1881–85 by 233.8.

The introduction of improvements in the iron industry since 1873 shows the tendency to adopt new devices in a time of financial depression.† When a business is profitable, there is no reason for stopping at a great loss each day to introduce better processes. In a time of depression, a stoppage is no loss. The cost of production of the coal, ore, and lime which enter into the production of pig iron, writes Mr. Joseph D. Weeks, has been lowered by the following agencies: —

The use of steam-drills instead of hand-drills, of coal-cutting machines for the pick of the miner, of compressed air in place of steam, of locomotive and water carriage in place of mules and of human carriage, of dynamite and its associate explosives in place of powder, of lime and water cartridges instead of powder cartridges, of the long-walled system of mining instead of the pillar and room, etc. In the blast furnaces there have been important changes in the lines of the furnaces,— in the methods of blowing and admitting the air, of charging the furnaces, of using the metal without allowing it to become cold, and of improved hoisting apparatus. In the rolling-mill, the improvements are almost without number. Some of them are growths; that is, a little change to-day, another change to-morrow, until in months' or years' time a gradual improvement has taken place, as compared with the years before, that would hardly be believed without making the comparison. I presume that, had I time, I could name at least five hundred improvements, some that have decreased cost and others that have improved quality.

Even in the case of improvements introduced before 1873, it has been only since then that their use has been applied on an extended scale. The manner in which improvements have lowered the price of iron illustrates the characteristics of modern industries in general.

* See, also, Appendix V.

† A few years after the panic of 1873, a large iron manufacturer, after lamenting the poor prospects in his industry, said, " And yet we were never making so many improvements as now."

The price of lead has fallen, as is well known, because of the extraordinary amount of lead liberated in treating the argentiferous lead ores discovered in Colorado, Montana, Nevada, Utah, and other Western States and Territories. The lead, being produced as secondary to the yield of silver, was sold for what it would bring,* regardless of the conditions affecting the mines worked solely for lead.

The effect on prices of a sudden opening of new supplies has never been more marked than in the matter of copper. The recent discovery of immense deposits in Arizona, Montana, and Spain has caused a revolution in this industry. The great yield in the West utterly overwhelmed the Lake Superior combination, which formerly controlled the market in the United States.† In the spring of 1882, copper here fell from twenty-two cents per pound in the spring of 1882 to only eleven and a half cents in 1885, solely from the causes named.

Tin has not fallen seriously in price. The average price in 1884 was about the same as for 1866–67 at Hamburg. The unusual speculation in metals about 1873 (see Chart II.) carried the price of tin higher than it had been for about forty years, so that the quotation for 1873 is 30 per cent. above the ordinary prices. Passing this by, however, the downward movement since 1873, so far as it exists, is fully accounted for by the discovery of large deposits of tin in New South Wales, Queensland, and Tasmania.‡

The great decline in the prices of English wool (the grade known as " Lincoln "), mohair, and alpaca has a

'* The white lead corroders west of the Mississippi getting their lead at so low a price, the corroders on the Atlantic seaboard were placed in a very critical position. The prices of paints, also, have thus greatly fallen of late.

† The Anaconda Mine in Montana led in the shipment to Europe of the vast excess of supply, and broke down the price abroad.

‡ See *Mineral Resources of the United States*, 1883–84. I am also indebted for information to Mr. R. W. Raymond, of New York.

curious cause. Before 1874, they were used on a vast scale in the manufacture of stiff, hard, and lustrous fabrics for ladies' wear, of which "alpaca" is a type. But, by a sudden freak of fashion, about 1874 these goods were wholly given up; and their place was taken by soft and pliable fabrics made from merino. The change was so marked as practically to destroy the demand * for English long-combing wools as well as for mohair and alpaca. The price of the fine wools, however, has been affected by the greatly increased product of Australia and South America.†

Cochineal gives another illustration of the changes in modern industries. Cochineal, for which an extensive demand formerly existed in dyeing and printing cloths, has been superseded by the aniline dyes, owing to the discovery of coloring materials in hydro-carbons, drawn chiefly from coal and petroleum. The yarn was weakened by cochineal, and spinners were glad enough to find that the cheaper aniline dyes gave as brilliant colors without weakening the yarn.

Nitrate of soda and saltpetre fell in price because of the excessive yield from the deposits of Western South America. The exportation of "Chili saltpetre" (nitrate of soda) has of late been larger than the world's consumption.‡ The average price for 1881–85 is about the same as for the years 1874–76. The article, however, is subject to great fluctuations of price.

---

* Lord Penzance, *Nineteenth Century*, September, 1886, says an English farmer who formerly received £1,400 for his yearly clip now gets only £600. For very careful tables of prices of English wools and for information, I am much indebted to Mr. George William Bond and to Mr. John L. Hayes.

† Leroy-Beaulieu, *ibid.*, p. 397, finds a close connection between the falling prices of fine wool and the shipments from Australia, the Cape, and La Plate. The number of bales imported in 1864 was 458,000; in 1868, 879,000; in 1877, 1,272,000; in 1885, 1,740,000.

‡ Wagner's *Jahresbericht* for 1884 states the facts as follows in metric tons : —

	1881.	1882.	1883.
Exports from South America, ...	319,000	410,000	530,000
World's consumption, ...	286,000	372,000	468,000

Coal varies greatly in price from time to time; but about 1873 it underwent an exceptional rise in price in England, while of late the production has been forced in an unusual way. In twenty years there has been an increase of 145 per cent. Apart from the improvements in mining already referred to, iron can be smelted with one-half the coal formerly required, and so requires less coal; while the growth of English stock companies has stimulated the activity of producers.

The industrial gains of society over nature are especially prominent in the case of paper. A pulp made from the fibre of wood, instead of rags, is used in its manufacture. Not only is the wood-pulp ground by machinery, but lately it is also prepared by a chemical process of decomposition. The latter variety is used for the better grades of paper. Of two kinds of book-paper which in 1873 were sold at seventeen and fourteen cents per pound in the United States, the price, owing to the new methods, has fallen one-half. The use of pulp, moreover, has cheapened the rags which are still partially used. Where the machine-made pulp is used, as in coarser kinds of paper, like newspaper stock, the fall in price is still more marked. Manufacturers, also, are learning how to use these processes to better effect; and the machinery is being steadily improved.

The supply of white-oak staves for the United States, since the Civil War, has been drawn from Arkansas and Tennessee, which have been penetrated by railways. This has made a vast difference in their price; but inferior wood is also used, which would have a similar effect on quotations.

Mahogany has been affected by exceptional influences. The chief supply formerly came from Cuba and San Domingo; but during the rebellion in Cuba, from 1868 to 1878, new sources of supply were sought for in Mexico, where operations were stimulated by the unusually high prices about 1873, due to scarcity. After the close of the rebellion, Cuba again furnished mahogany; and her exportations have since been increasing. This is sufficient to account for the fall in price, apart from the fact that inferior wood affects the quotations.

The fall in the prices of iron and steel, and all materials entering into the manufacture of railroad cars, together with improvements in the tools and process of manufacture, will, in the United States, account for any decline in the price of cars. The increase of strength, moreover, makes a great difference in the weight to be carried, so that the superiority of the new cars has caused a depreciation in the value of the old ones.*

The marked progress of improvements is also seen in the making of boots and shoes. In 1870, the operative was also a skilled shoemaker: now, he is known only as an edge-trimmer, an edge-setter, or a laster, because machinery has been introduced which performs a special part of the manufacture. One machine trims the sole, another the heel, another polishes the shoe; another, a beating-out machine, disposes of a whole row of shoes instead of one, as in former days. The button-holes are now worked by a machine which enables one operative to make five thousand in a day. In the McKay sewing-machine, on which four hundred pairs were sewed in a day, a small arm made two movements to throw one loop of thread over the needle; but, when it occurred to the inventors to cause the arm to throw one loop at each movement, the operative was enabled to sew eight hundred to one thousand pairs in a day.† Such changes are constantly going on, and it is little marvel that shoes are better made and lower in price.

---

*I am indebted for information to Professor Arthur T. Hadley and to Mr. M. N. Forney, Secretary of the Master Car-builders' Association, New York.

†The Goodyear McKay welt machine sews the welt on to the upper leather, and then sews the outer sole on to the welt, giving practically the advantages of hand-sewed work at a less price.

The fall of prices shown by Mr. Goschen can thus, without a question, be explained by causes other than the scarcity of gold. The course of progress, moreover, has gone farther and in more directions than I have space to describe * here. Suffice it to conclude with the facts in regard to the lowering of charges for transportation, which affect the prices of a great range of commodities. The average rates of freight for wheat from Chicago to New York † have fallen to less than 40 per cent. of the rates of 1873, whether we refer to transit by rail or canal. The charges for ocean transportation have fallen quite as much.‡ One of the mechanical triumphs of recent years has been the transformation of the old steamship into the new,§ which, taken in connection with the improved grain elevators and various expedients for receiving and discharging cargoes, has warranted the statement that a single sailor to-day transports two times as much as he did in 1870, three times as much as in 1860, and four

---

* As illustrations, we may point to the character of the improvements introduced in the making of glass (which led to the labor riots at Charleroi in Belgium). One new Siemens "tank furnace" does the work of eight old coal furnaces, while it requires only four men instead of twenty-eight. Common window glass has consequently fallen in price one-half. (See Fowler, *Appreciation of Gold*, p. 39.) Again, steel rails can now be made at a less price than iron rails were made a few years ago, owing to well-known inventions. Still, again, in the cotton mills, spindles which revolved four thousand times in a minute about 1873 now revolve ten thousand times in a minute.

In connection with the great increase of supplies, see a suggestive investigation by Mr. Luke Hansard, in the *Report of the Royal Commission on the Depression of Trade*, Appendix, pp. 405–414.

† *United States Bureau of Statistics*, January, 1885.

‡ See *Contemporary Review*, April, 1885, p. 545, where Fowler gives the charges from Calcutta on jute, wheat, linseed, and rape-seed, from 1881 to 1884. See, also, Leroy-Beaulieu, *ibid.*, p. 401 ; Fowler, *Appreciation of Gold*, pp. 45, 71 ; *The Public*, December 22, 1881.

§ The improved ship, being a better and cheaper carrying instrument, is itself the cause of the depreciation in value of older ships. In fact, this is the natural result of improvements. This depreciation of capitalized property, owing to improvements, is Mr. Frewen's real difficulty, and is not explained by the scarcity of gold.

times as much as in 1850. The fall in the rates of freight from Calcutta to London would alone account for the fall in price of several articles in Mr. Goschen's list. The tolls and pilotage on the Suez Canal * have fallen about one-third since 1873.

The steady extension of the electric telegraph, together with changes in methods of doing business, helps to lower the cost of production of many commodities. The means of instant communication with agents and correspondents in opposite parts of the world wholly obviates the carrying of large stocks of goods, and economizes the use of capital like a labor-saving machine. The whole world is thus opened to any dealer, and the middle-man is less used than formerly. Producers are brought nearer to consumers.

Of the fall of prices in his table, Mr. Goschen says, " I am bound to say it appears to me that these figures reveal an extraordinary state of things " ; and he thinks it is due to the scarcity of gold. It has been shown conclusively, however, that, in every case investigated, a cause peculiar to the commodity has been found, without the need of referring to a general cause connected with gold. The opening of better lands to cultivation, the discovery of richer mineral deposits, the perfection and cheapening of transportation by which all these distant resources have become easily available, the increased mobility of labor and capital in finding out these new resources, the steady and extraordinary development of mechanical and chemical improvements in a great number of industries,— these are some of the main causes † which have affected the prices of a variety of commodities since 1873.

---

* Leroy-Beaulieu, *ibid.*, p. 4.

† Courcelle-Seneuil (*Journal des Économistes*, August, 1886, p. 163) finds that the completion of a period within which productive railways can be built has had an important influence in lowering prices since 1883.

Laveleye, however, remarks * that improvements made
even greater progress in the years 1860–70 than they have
since then ; but that prices in the former period rose from
18 to 20 per cent. Why, then, he urges, can the same
cause have produced an opposite effect since 1873 ? To
this, it must be said, If improvements multiplied before
1873, and yet the prices of the commodities affected did
not fall, the expected result must have been masked or
counteracted by other influences. Surely, no one will con-
tend for a moment that improved processes in particular
industries will not lower the value of commodities relatively to gold, if gold has remained unchanged in its conditions of production. This would lead one to suppose
that the prices of many articles before 1873 must have
shown a fall, had it not been for the vast extension of
speculation and overtrading and the influences of the new
gold. But, now that the inflation and abnormal conditions of the previous period have been left behind, the
effect of improvements has become more clearly apparent.
In fact, when one considers that, with all the unparalleled
development of cheapening processes since 1850 in almost every industry which ministers to human wants,
prices are no lower or, by the Hamburg figures, even
10 per cent. above the level of prices in 1847–50, one is
penetrated by the conviction that prices are still buoyed
up by the high tide of an abundant gold supply. Else
why should prices not be much lower than in 1850 ? " If,
under such circumstances," says Cairnes,† " prices did

---

* *Contemporary Review*, May, 1886, p. 621.

† " A rise in the price of commodities, if general, implies commonly a fall
in the value of money ; but, according to the ordinary use of language, alike
by economists and in common speech, money would, I apprehend, in certain
circumstances, be said to have fallen in value, even though the prices of large
classes of commodities remained unaffected. For example, supposing improvements to have been effected in some branch of production, resulting in
a diminished cost of the commodity, the value of money remaining the same,
prices would fall. If, under such circumstances, prices did not fall, that
could only be because money had not remained the same, but had fallen in

not fall, that could only be because money had not remained the same, but had fallen in value." Or it would
be more correct to say that the cost of producing money
had fallen; for, if prices are now nearly the same as in
1850, in reality the cost of production of both commodities and money has fallen, leaving them relatively to each
other in very much the same position as in the beginning.
When we once fully apprehend the influences of the
progress of society on prices, we cannot admit that a
fall of prices is connected in any necessary way with a
scarcity of gold.

§ VI.   The preceding discussion, however, does not
account for a general fall in prices. If the fall of prices
has been general, it might suggest a single cause affecting
all commodities, such as the scarcity of the medium by
which goods are exchanged. In fact, it seems to be quite
necessary to a theory which explains the fall in prices
by the scarcity of gold that the fall should be universal.
And this is so stated. "The most disastrous characteristic," remarks Mr. Giffen,* "of the recent fall of prices
has been the *descent all round* to a lower range than that
of which there had been any previous experience." In
the case of English exports and imports, the reader will
find in Appendix V. a large collection of commodities
which have actually risen in price since 1873, although
that was a year of abnormally high prices. Mr. Pal-

---

value. The continuance of prices unaltered would, therefore, under such circumstances, amount to proof of a fall in the value of gold. Now, when, in
connection with this consideration, we take account of the fact that over the
greater portion of the field of British industry improvement is constantly taking place, it is obvious that the mere movements of prices here, taken without
reference to the conditions of production, are no sure criterion of changes in
the value of gold." *Essays*, p. 106.

* *Contemporary Review*, June, 1885, p. 809. This is the ground taken by
Laveleye, *Contemporary Review*, May, 1886, p. 621. Frewen (*Nineteenth Century*, October, 1885, p. 601) says: "Prices have *all fallen* more than twenty per
cent. . . . Prices *all round* are falling lower and lower still, because that circulating medium which measures values has diminished."

grave * points out a rise in price in 1886, as compared
with 1881, of six of the articles used in the *Economist*
table. Moreover, in the same list, comparing the period
before 1875 with that since 1880, sugar, tea, tobacco,
butcher's meat, raw silk, and leather have been at times
higher in the latter than in the former period.

The Hamburg tables also give additional evidence that
prices are not all moving in the same direction. I have
collected † twenty-one articles, out of the one hundred
quoted at Hamburg, which show an upward tendency,
by comparing the average prices of 1881–85 with those
of 1871–75. The average of the numbers representing
the prices of these twenty-one articles in the period 1871–
75 was 164.2, and in 1881–85 183.8. In the same lists
there can be found at least twenty-one articles ‡ which
have shown a decided tendency to fall in price. The
remaining articles do not show a marked movement in
either direction. Forsell § makes an interesting analysis
of the whole one hundred into two groups, classifying
those which show a tendency to rise and those which
show a tendency to fall. In the first class he includes
fifty-one articles, and in the second forty-nine articles,
with the following results in averages : —

	1847–50.	1851–60.	1861–70.	1871–75.	1876–80.	1881–85.
I.	100	125.3	130.3	147.1	143.7	146.4
II.	100	109.7	114.6	121.7	103.7	96.7

* *Report of the Royal Commission*, 1886, Appendix, p. 330. The articles are
Jamaica rum, potatoes, flax, hemp, ashes, and tin (although tin is quoted by
Mr. Goschen as showing a great decline in 1883).

	1871–75.	1881–85.		1871–75.	1881–85.
Malt, .	140.7	143.5	Almonds,	111.1	127 5
Buckwheat,	131.7	135.5	Wine, . .	221.9	284 1
Hops, .	339.4	355.3	Champagne,	121.2	124.5
Veal, .	153.1	183.9	Cocoa, . .	156.8	230.1
Mutton, .	135.4	158.1	Pepper, .	229.7	233.8
Pork, . .	126.7	126.9	Allspice, .	60.4	72.1
Butter,	188.3	191.6	Rum, .	181.8	199.1
Bristles, .	201.9	225.9	Ivory, . .	185.0	194.3
Buffalo horns,	184.9	235.9	Flax, . .	123.1	128.2
Herring, .	149.8	165.8	Gum elastic, . .	141.6	157.9
Dried fish, .	163.3	184.1			

‡ Wheat, flour, rape-seed oil, linseed oil, olive oil, palm oil, allspice, rice,
sago, cochineal, logwood, quicksilver, salt, chalk, silk, wool, potash, pearl-
ash, soda, stearine candles, and wax.

§ *The Appreciation of Gold*, etc., p. 22.

Whether to draw inferences as to a scarcity of gold from forty-nine articles, or to infer that gold was abundant, according to the prices of fifty-one articles, is an awkward dilemma for those who think that prices give direct evidence as to the quantity of money. As Forsell remarks, the theory of a scarcity of gold is incompatible with the rise * in price of so many commodities.

The purchasing power of gold, moreover, has been indicated in other ways, such as the higher prices paid for services, domestic servants, rents for houses, and for a vast number of things which, in their nature, cannot be included in price-lists, but which absorb a large part of every one's expenditure.

§ VII.   From the foregoing statements, it must be evident that the connection between prices and the quantity of gold is not so simple as some would have us suppose. But Mr. Goschen and his followers see reasons, in the direct and visible demands for gold, since silver was demonetized by Germany, to believe that gold † must be scarce enough to cause a general decline in prices.

Gold to the amount of nearly £200,000,000 has been required for supplying Germany, the United States, and Italy with new gold currencies.‡   This extraordinary demand fell on a diminished supply.

---

* Mr. Giffen (*Journal of Statistical Society*, March, 1879, p. 306) refers to the rise in price of textiles and metals (and their manufactures) in 1861–65, their fall in 1865–68, their rise again in 1868–73, and their fall again in 1873–79; and yet he cannot claim that there was any such corresponding changes in the quantity of gold in the world.   Such fluctuations drove Mulhall (*Contemporary Review*, August, 1885) to the extreme of asserting the absence of any connection whatever between prices and the quantity of gold.   See, also, the irregularity of movement in the prices in Bourne's table, *Journal of Statistical Society, ibid.*, pp. 411, 412.

† *Journal of Institute of Bankers*, May, 1883, p. 302.   Giffen (*Contemporary Review*, June, 1885, p. 815) computes the demand in the previous thirteen years of Germany at £80,000,000, of the United States at £82,000,000 (£34,-000,000 for imports less exports and £48,000,000 for home production), and of Italy at £20,000,000.

‡ Laveleye (*Contemporary Review*, May, 1886, p. 625) sees in the coinage by various countries since 1873 a cause for alarm.   The coinage of £220,000,000

The annual production of gold during the first five years after the discoveries of 1851 averaged nearly £30,000,000. It now amounts to less than £20,000,000. The new demand has been equal to the total supply of ten years. At the same time, we have to reckon with the normal demand for arts and manufactures,* while more gold has also been required to meet the wants of an increasing population and an increased balance of transactions in all gold-using countries.

No evidence is before us to prove that a fresh development of banking expedients has to such an extent further economized the use of gold as to neutralize this normal rate of increase. On the contrary, it is believed that, in England alone, the gold circulation has grown by £20,000,000 in ten years.

Now, if the existing stock of gold in the world, increased as it has been since 1850, has not been capable of meeting the demands specified by Mr. Goschen, in what way would the effects of a scarcity manifest themselves? If the insufficient quantity of gold has lowered prices, the process must have shown itself at some point in the machinery by which commodities are exchanged. Fortu-

---

since that year he states to be equal to the production of ten years. It is impossible, however, to judge of the demand for gold by the amounts coined, because there are received at the mints foreign and domestic coins, which should not be counted twice; and old plate is also brought to be coined. Mulhall probably overstates the case when he says (*Contemporary Review*, August, 1885) the annual average coinage of the world, 1870–84, was £14,000,000, of which one-half came from recoinage of old coins. One-fifth of the United States gold coinage in 1885 was from foreign coins and jewellers' has, plate, etc., to the amount of about $10,000,000. At least, the coinage since 1873 is not a demand additional to that referred to by Mr. Goschen. But, when Laveleye (*ibid.*, pp. 626, 627) refers to the falling off in the coinage of gold and silver since 1879 in England and France as evidence of a scarcity of gold, he forgets that this is, on the very surface, a reason for believing that the coinage is already so plentiful that no more is called for in these countries.

*Soetheer (*Materialien*, p. 38) places the annual consumption of gold in the arts at 90,000 kilograms, or nearly $60,000,000, and of silver at 515,000 kilograms, or about $21,000,000. An abundance of gold, however, will not affect the demand for plate, etc., by lowering the price of such articles; for the price in gold would not change.

nately, Mr. Giffen * gives an explanation as to how this
scarcity of gold has made itself felt: —

> A sudden pressure on the stock of the precious metals at a given
> period tends to disturb the money markets of the countries using
> them, makes money dear, or creates a steady apprehension that it
> may at any moment become dear, and so, by weakening the specu-
> lation in commodities and making it really difficult for merchants
> and traders to hold the stocks they would otherwise hold, contracts
> business and assists a fall in prices.

And, later,† he asserts that

> The rate of discount and the interest of money do not depend on
> the scarcity or abundance of "money," using the term in its strict
> sense, but on the scarcity or abundance of capital relative to the
> demands of borrowers.

As a consequence, Mr. Giffen, in looking over the years
since 1871, has been struck with the succession of stringencies in the money market directly traceable to the
difficulty of getting gold. Now, curiously enough, the
period before 1873 was more remarkable for these disturbances than was the succeeding period. From 1855 to
1873, the rate at the Bank of England rose beyond 6
per cent. eleven times, and twice to 10 per cent.; at the
Bank of France, for the same years, the rate rose above
5 per cent. ten times, and once to 9 per cent.; at the
Bank of Germany, it rose six times beyond 6 per cent.,
and once to 9 per cent. There must have been great
difficulty in getting gold before 1873, if we are to judge
from the frequency and intensity of the disturbances in
the money market. But there is no corresponding evidence as to a scarcity of gold to be drawn from such dis-

---

* *Journal of Statistical Society*, June, 1879, p. 49. He claims, also (*ibid.*,
p. 445), that, after a fall in prices due to a scarcity of gold, there is an apparent
superabundance of gold, due to the lower range of prices. Or, as Laveleye
puts it, "the more rare it [gold] becomes, the more it apparently exceeds the
demand" (*Contemporary Review*, May, 1886, p. 631).

† *Contemporary Review*, June, 1885, p. 816.

turbances since 1873.*   In fact, in the very machinery of borrowing and lending, where any such change might show itself, there is no evidence whatever of a scarcity of gold.

In order to test this question thoroughly, I have compiled † the following table, which shows the total note circulation and the amount and character of the specie reserves in all the principal banks of Europe and the United States (000 omitted) : —

	1870–1874.			1885.		
	Reserves.		Total note circulation.	Reserves.		Total note circulation.
	Gold.	Silver.		Gold.	Silver.	
Banks of the United Kingdom, ...	[1872] $153,825		$198,540	$141,205		$186,850
Banks of Australia, .	[1874] 41,380		20,580	65,890		28,115
Bank of France, . .	[1869] 131,800	$106,600	274,100	231,483	$217,087	583,010
Banks of Italy, . . .	[1870] 15,447	33,695	88,487	56,121	11,203	189,690
National Bank of Belgium, ...	[1870] 4,893	14,230	40,505	13,900	6,540	73,400
Bank of the Netherlands, ...	[1871] 2,109	55,320	62,857	19,161	38,366	76,972
Bank of Austria-Hungary, ...	[1871] 16,651	37,160	119,000	25,902	48,646	136,351
Imperial State Bank of Russia, ...	[1871] 80,361	4,775	429,486	102,207	676	429,860
Imperial Bank of Sweden, ...	[1870] 1,749	4,325	7,327	3,436	777	9,835
Bank of Norway, . .	[1873] 7,058	1,535	11,794	7,169		9,287
National Bank of Denmark, ...	[1872] 3,801	6,980	16,877	11,566	846	18,370
National Banks of the United States, . . .	[1871] 18,900		284,561	158,100	7,900	276,500
Total, ...	$477,974	$264,620	$1,554,114	$836,140	$332,041	$2,018,840

From these figures, it will be seen that the reserves in the banks of the civilized world show a very remark-

---

* At the Bank of England, since 1873, the rate has never been higher than 6 per cent. and for only ninety-six days in all, divided between four occasions (in 1874, 1875, 1878, and 1882). At the Bank of France, in the same time, the rate has never risen higher than 5 per cent., and for one hundred and ninety days, divided between three occasions (in 1874, 1881, and 1882). At the Bank of Germany, also, the rate has never risen higher than 6 per cent., and for one hundred and thirty-seven days, divided between four occasions (in 1874, 1875, 1876, and 1882). See *Report of Royal Commission on Depression of Trade*, Appendix, pp. 370–373.

† From figures given by Soetbeer, *Materialien*, etc., pp. 58–70. For France, see *Bulletin de Statistique Comparée*, January, 1887, pp. 62, 63.

able increase in gold. Although the total note circulation was increased 29 per cent., the gold in the reserves was increased 75 per cent., while the silver was also increased 25 per cent. In 1870–74, the gold reserves amounted to 28 per cent. of the total note circulation, and constituted 64 per cent. of all the specie reserves. In 1885, the gold bore a larger ratio to a larger issue of paper, or 41 per cent. of the total note circulation; and, in spite of unusual accumulations of silver (in the Bank of France, for example), the gold formed 71 per cent. of the specie reserves. This is a very significant showing. What it means, without a shadow of doubt, is that the supply of gold is so abundant that the character and safety of the note circulation have been improved in a signal manner. In 1871–74 there was $1 of gold for every $3.60 of paper circulation.* In 1885 there was $1 of gold for every $2.40.

There are, moreover, strong and substantial reasons for believing, on independent grounds, that gold is abundant instead of scarce. When we compare the total production since 1850 with that since 1492, the result is very striking, and cannot be too strongly emphasized: —

	Gold.	Silver.
1493–1850,	$3,314,550,000	$7,358,450,000
1851–1885,	4,452,525,000	2,399,475,000

In the last thirty-five years, one and one-third times as much gold has been produced as in the three hundred and fifty-eight years† preceding 1850, while only one-third

---

* In the face of these facts, Frewen's statement (*ibid.*, p. 597) seems a little wide of the mark: "Not only does the note currency diminish as the gold represented by such currency diminishes, but, . . . as gold becomes scarcer and prices tend to fall, so also does the entire system of credit continue to contract." Cernuschi, the very apostle of bimetallism, himself admits that "the fall in prices which is complained of is not due to what has been called a scarcity of gold,— a scarcity which is purely imaginary." London *Economist*, April 24, 1886.

† The amount in existence in 1848 is only a matter of conjecture. The estimates vary from $1,000,000,000 to $3,150,000,000.

as much silver has been produced in the same time. And yet we hear a great deal of the phenomenal yield of the silver mines of late years. What has become of this vast quantity of gold? We are fairly obliged to explain why gold has not fallen in value. It certainly would have fallen, had not its use been extended; and, out of the extraordinary addition to the world's supply, the demands of France, India, Germany, Italy, and the United States have been easily met. The countries of the world are yet saturated with the new gold.* Mr. Goschen speaks of an addition to England's gold circulation in ten years of $100,000,000; while, strangely enough, Mr. Giffen is alarmed because there was no coinage at all in 1881–82! Laveleye, also, is troubled because the coinage in France is diminishing!

But we hear it said constantly that the annual production of gold is falling off, and that its value must rise. Now, this is what Mr. S. Dana Horton† calls the "sempiternal object of erroneous reasoning." The value of gold is affected by the total existing supply, which is very large relatively to the annual supply. And yet it is true that the annual production has fallen off from its highest point, about 1853. Before 1840, the annual production of gold amounted to about $14,000,000 : it rose as high as $157,000,000; but in 1885 it was about $100,000,000. A millionnaire, however, does not feel poor because his annual increase of wealth is a few thousands less than it was at its greatest: his past accumulations are still his, and his yearly income is yet large. The yield from the

---

* Söetbeer (*Materialien*, p. 70) gives the following summary of the amount of gold in the civilized countries by years (in millions of dollars) : —

1877.	1878.	1879.	1880.	1881.	1882.	1883.	1884.	1885.
722	712	875	947	975	1,017	1,150	1,170	1,260

† *Quarterly Journal of Economics*, October, 1885, p. 58. Laveleye and Disraeli are addicted to the "sempiternal" fallacy. (See *Contemporary Review*, May, 1886, p. 623.) Cernuschi, however, remarks, "The power of the gramme of gold is proportionate to the whole of the gold, . . . not to the importance of the annual production." *Anatomy of Money*, p. 11.

mines to-day is enormous compared with any period previous to 1850, and this has been kept up for thirty-five
years. The longer this continues, the less important will
be the variations in the annual supply.*

§ VIII. Even though the gold production from 1850
to 1885 has been great enough to meet very heavy demands, yet it may be asked how far have the means for
economizing money developed of late. Mr. Giffen believes
no evidence exists as to an extension of credit devices
since 1873, that England and the United States were
already fully " banked" before this period, and that the
clearing-system on the continent shows no progress. The
increase in population and commodities, he urges, has not
only not been compensated for by any economizing expedients, but the increased demand for gold has fallen on
a diminishing supply.

To examine, first, whether the issue of notes has saved
the use of gold in the principal countries of the world
since 1873, it will be necessary to compare the amounts
of uncovered paper, not the amounts of the total circulation in the periods taken. To the extent, of course, to
which the covered circulation has increased, no extension
of credit has taken place. For this purpose, I have prepared a table showing the amounts of the total circulation, and the amounts of the total circulation less the

* The annual average production of gold and silver since 1850 is as follows:

Periods.	Gold.	Silver.
1851–55	$139,077,000	$40,096,750
1856–60	140,729,000	41,177,250
1861–65	129,081,000	49,827,000
1866–70	136,035,000	59,924,000
1871–75	121,302,000	86,162,000
1876–80	120,261,000	95,515,500
1881–85	104,025,000	107,190,000

The yield for the single years since 1880 is as follows: —

	Gold.	Silver.
1881	$110,810,000	$98,418,000
1882	103,564,000	105,916,000
1883	100,822,000	108,582,000
1884	101,940,000	110,899,000

Soetbeer, *Materialien*, p. 1.

specie reserves, in the principal countries for the years
1870–74 and for 1885 (000 omitted) : —

Countries.	1870–74.		1885.	
	Uncovered by specie.	Total circulation.	Uncovered by specie.	Total circulation.
Great Britain,* . .	[1872] $44,719	$216,939	$45,644	$211,139
France,† . . .	[1869] 39,739	322,869	135,041	583,610
Italy,‡	[1870] 168,000	180,000	170,000	285,200
Austria-Hungary,§ . . .	[1873] 209,678	263,616	188,646	263,194
Germany,‖ . . .	[1871] 135,750	312,649	124,500	299,905
Russia,¶	[1873] 339,652	475,357	525,000	627,000
United States,** . . .	[1871] 505,400	505,400	172,000	814,300
Total, ...	$1,442,938	$2,276,830	$1,360,831	$3,084,348

From these figures, it will be seen that in 1885, as compared with the years about 1873, the uncovered circulation decreased by $82,000,000, or 5 per cent.; while the
total circulation increased by $800,000,000, or 35 per cent.
This indicates quite clearly the effects of the great
addition to the world's stock of gold and silver since

* Soetbeer, *Materialien*, p. 59, and Statistical Abstract, 1884.

† The mean of the highest and the lowest circulation is given for 1869.
See *Bulletin de Statistique Comparée*, iii., 21, and London *Economist*, January
23 and December 25, 1869. For 1885, see Soetbeer, *ibid.*, p. 73.

‡ See *Relazione sulla Circolazione Cartacea*, made to the Italian Chamber of
Deputies, March 15, 1875, Appendix, pp. 20, 41; and Haupt, *L'Histoire Moné-
taire de notre Temps*, p. 274.

§ See Soetbeer, *ibid.*, pp. 64, 74; and Mülinen, *Finances de l'Autriche*, p. 163.

‖ For 1871, the uncovered circulation is given by Soetbeer, *ibid.*, p. 74.
Taking the total circulation of all the German banks (given for 1871, p. 65),
and supposing the *Landespapiergeld* to be the same in 1871 as in 1870, I get
the total circulation for the year 1871 instead of 1870.

¶ See *Bulletin de Statistique Comparée*, ii., 161; Haupt, *ibid.*, p. 366; and
Soetbeer, *ibid.*, pp. 66, 75.

** For 1871, from the 674,000,000 of United States notes and National Bank
notes there has been deducted $168,600,000 for notes held by the treasury and
the banks. No notes could be presented for specie in 1871. For 1885, from
$664,000,000 of United States notes and National Bank notes, $134,800,000 was
deducted for notes held by the treasury and the banks. The amount of specie
which could be drawn on by holders of either kinds of notes, to the amount of
$278,400,000 gold and $79,000,000 silver, was also deducted, to ascertain the
uncovered note circulation. Cf. *Finance Report*, 1886, i., p. lxxx.

1873. Specie to the amount of $800,000,000 has gone into circulation in the form of note issues, representing an equivalent amount of specie ; but gold has not been economized by the use of credit in the form of notes. While the total circulation of these countries has increased 35 per cent., the paper has been much better protected ; for in 1870–74 the specie was but 36 per cent. of the total issues, and in 1885 the specie was 55 per cent. of the total issues. From this table, then, we see where the gold referred to by Mr. Goschen has gone. About $750,000,000 of specie, mostly gold, has gone into circulation since 1873, in the form of covered paper issues, in the United States and Italy alone. The paper currency of every country except Russia has gained in security, together with a large increase in many of the countries. The gold supplies have not merely permitted an enlarged note circulation, but have furnished a much better protection to that increased issue.

In regard to the use of checks and clearing-houses in economizing the use of money, Mr. Giffen is probably correct in saying that this system had attained its full growth in the United States and Great Britain before 1873 ; but an important conclusion is to be drawn from this. Just to the extent to which the system may have been perfected is it one which expands with the expansion of business. In the same proportion that transactions increase, this means of economizing the use of money will (approximately) increase. The clearing-system, in fact, is one which grows with the work to be done.* Certainly,

---

* How well this is recognized may be seen by the accepted custom of measuring the extent of business by the figures of the clearings. "The returns of the London Clearing-house," says Mr. Palgrave, "may be regarded as indicating approximately the value of the business of the country as indicated by price." *Report of Royal Commission*, Appendix, p. 330. In the United States, of all the receipts by the 1,966 national banks on one day in 1881, 95 per cent. were made up of forms of credit, exclusive even of circulating notes ; while in New York City this percentage was 98.7. At all the banks, only .65 of 1

this is true of wholesale transactions; while in retail trade the use of checks is steadily widening. An elastic system, so far as it is ready to perform exchanges in proportion to their increase, meets the need of more money the moment it appears. If there has been no increase in clearings under such conditions, it only shows that transactions have not increased, not that there is any less efficacy in the system. Where checks are in general use, other forms of credit are of less importance.*

On the continent, the borrower at a bank will, as a rule, prefer notes instead of the right to draw on a deposit by checks. Yet, even at the Bank of France, 66 per cent. of the transactions in 1877–78 were effected without the use of notes and coin.† But, on the other hand, the *Chambre de Compensation*, established in Paris in 1872–73 (including twelve of the large banks), with the help of the Bank of France, performed exchanges ‡ the first year to the value of \$320,000,000, which in 1883–84 had risen only as high as \$843,000,000. Clearing-houses were also established in Austria and Italy in 1872, but they have made little gain. The exchanges at the *Saldirungs-verein* in Vienna (formed by the four old banks of the Saldosaal of 1864, together with ten other large banks) were no greater in 1885 than in 1872, being at that time about \$200,000,000 a year. The clearings of the *Stanze di Compenzatione*

---

per cent. of gold was used; and, in New York City, only .27 of 1 per cent. of gold was used. See *Report of the Comptroller of the Currency*, 1881, p. 14. Cf. also *Journal Statistical Society*, June, 1865, " Country Clearings."

* The use of bills of exchange in Great Britain seems to be falling off, with an increased use of checks. Cf. Sauerbeck, *Prices of Commodities*, p. 8.

† Cf. *Journal of Statistical Society*, 1884, p. 493. If Mulhall's *Dictionary of Statistics* can be trusted, the banking of the world since 1840 has increased elevenfold,—three times faster than commerce, and thirty times faster than population. Leroy-Beaulieu reports that "checks have become everywhere a more common instrument of payment " (*Revue des Deux Mondes*, May, 1886, p. 403).

‡ The figures for the continent are taken from Rauchberg's *Die Entwickelung des Clearing-verkehres*, in the *Bulletin de l'Institut International de Statistique*, i., p. 140, etc.

in the several cities of Italy show a gain from $129,000,-000 in 1883 to $348,000,000 in 1885, with some promise for the future. But, in Germany, a decisive advance was made in 1883, under the leadership of the Reichsbank, in the establishment of clearing-houses in Berlin, Hamburg, Frankfort, Bremen, Cologne, Leipzig, Stuttgart, Breslau, and Dresden. In the year 1884, the exchanges amounted to the large sum of $3,032,000,000. Although not so large as the $30,000,000,000 a year in New York or London, it is a very promising increase in the means of economizing the use of specie on the continent.

In the international trade, also, as Leroy-Beaulieu * suggests, it is not necessary that the precious metals should increase as rapidly as commerce expands. The ocean and land telegraph, the shortening of routes by canals, and the extraordinary improvements in the ocean steamships have resulted in economizing the shipments of gold between different countries. A few years ago, twelve or fifteen days were taken up in carrying gold from New York to London ; but now six days are sufficient. Formerly, gold was ninety days coming from Australia to England ; while only thirty-five days are now required. In this way, gold being a less time in passing from person to person in international transactions, greater rapidity of circulation is insured, with all the effects of an increase in quantity.† The use of foreign bills of exchange is as great as ever between bankers in different countries ;

---

* *Revue des Deux Mondes*, May, 1886, p. 402. This is more or less confirmed by Bourne's table (*Journal of Statistical Society*, 1879, p. 411).

† Fowler (*Appreciation of Gold*, pp. 12, 13) says of English trade : " The total of our imports and exports from 1866 to 1875 was in round figures £6,000,-000,000, and the total of bullion and specie imported and exported was, in the same period, £530,000,000 ; but the total of our imports and exports from 1876 to 1885 was £6,700,000,000, and this vast amount was moved with the aid of £493,000,000 of bullion and specie. If we take the gold alone, we used about £327,000,000 in the former decade against £278,000,000 in the latter." If we can trust Mulhall, in 1861-70 the amount of the precious metals transported was 12 per cent. of the sea-borne commerce of the world, while in 1871-80 it was only 8 per cent.

while there is far greater activity of late in the trans-
mission of securities which discharge international liabilities as well as in the extended use of international money
orders.*

§ IX. To get more light on the question whether gold
has risen relatively to all commodities from causes affecting gold itself, it would be profitable to examine into the
movement of prices in India; † but this will be deferred
until it can be discussed more fully.

It will be as well to close the present study by referring
briefly to the argument of the English writers,‡ that a
scarcity of gold has brought about a fall in rents, profits,
and wages. It will be recalled at once, in regard to rents,
that a marked characteristic of the period since 1873 has
been the opening up of new and fertile lands, whose products have been transported at a greatly diminished rate.
But this in itself is a reason why lands in the older
countries should be thrown out of cultivation, and why
rents should be lowered. This phenomenon, then, can be
accounted for on other grounds than the scarcity of gold.

In attributing the fall in the rate of profits to the
general fall of prices (due to a single cause, the scarcity
of gold), these writers fall into an error which has been
already thoroughly exposed by Mr. Mill,§ who pointed

---

* In the countries composing the Postal Union in 1885, the issue of international money orders had risen to $60,000,000, and the issue of domestic
money orders to the surprising amount of $1,821,000,000. See *Statistique
Générale du Service Postal*, Berne, 1886. In the United States alone domestic
money orders have increased $80,000,000 since 1873. I am much indebted for
information to Mr. C. F. Macdonald, of the Post-office Department.

† These prices, so far as published, can be found in Barbour's *Theory of
Bimetallism;* in J. E. O'Conor's *Report on Prices and Wages in India*, 1886,
Government of India, Department of Finance and Commerce; and in the
Report of the Royal Commission on Depression of Trade, Appendix, pp. 331-342,
378-382.

‡ Frewen, *ibid.*, p. 599; Giffen, *Journal of Statistical Society*, 1879, p. 57,
and *Contemporary Review*, June, 1885, p. 816; the writer in the *Edinburgh
Review*, July, 1886, p. 39; and Sauerbeck, *ibid.*, p. 42.

§ *Principles of Political Economy*, B. IV., chap. iv., § 1.

out that "the fall of price, which if confined to one commodity really does lower the profits of the producer, ceases to have that effect as soon as it extends to all commodities." In some industries, however, owing to changes in relative demand and supply, intense competition has set in since 1873, and producers have necessarily submitted to lowered profits. But, in so far as prices have fallen in all industries alike, that cannot have been the cause of a general fall of profits.

If, however, labor has not fallen in price, while other things have fallen, "what has really taken place," says Mr. Mill, in the connection already quoted, "is a rise of wages; and it is that, and not the fall of prices, which has lowered the profits of capital." It is quite certain that there has been no fall of real wages since 1873, while there is good reason to suppose that they have risen.* In the United States, money wages may have fallen slightly in some industries; but an allowance must be made for the depreciation of paper previous to 1879. American producers have been enabled to sell at lower prices, and yet pay relatively higher wages, only by a gain in efficiency. As a typical case, the accompanying facts are furnished me by a manufacturer from his own books: —

	Average wages per day.	Amount paid for a given piece of work.
December, 1867.	$2.05	$1.00
" 1876.	1.71	.78½
" 1886.	1.79	.37₁₀

For Germany, Soetbeer gives a variety of evidence to show the rise of wages † since 1873. Money wages in Italy,‡ which were indicated by the number 179 in 1873,

---

* See *Report of Massachusetts Bureau of Labor Statistics* for 1884, and *Report on the Statistics of Wages*, United States Census, 1880, vol. xx.

† *Materialien*, pp. 88, 90, 91.

‡ See *Movimento dei Prezzi di Alcuni Generi Alimentari dal 1862 al 1885* (1886), issued by the Italian Department of Agriculture, p. xxvii.

were in 1884 expressed by 222. But it is not necessary to cite further evidence on this point. The fact that wages have risen tends to confirm the belief that the fall of prices is due chiefly to the introduction of improvements.

§ X. In the study of this subject, we have been confronted at the outset with a fall of prices since 1873 which happened to coincide with the demonetization of silver by Germany and the United States, and the beginning of a new epoch in the production of many commodities. To assume that because the fall of prices coincided with the demonetization of silver it was due to an appreciation of gold, without considering whether the coincident phenomena were traceable to entirely distinct causes, is to fall into the fallacy of *post hoc propter hoc*. The forces which fix the level of prices at any time, moreover, are far too complex to admit of the inference that, because prices have fallen seriously, gold has become scarce. On the other hand, all the phenomena presented to show the scarcity of gold are explicable on other grounds.

But — what is of very grave importance — we must admit that great changes in prices may take place irrespective of the scarcity or abundance of the precious metals. From this, it follows that, as a standard of payment for contracts, neither gold nor silver, nor even gold and silver (if they should ever be firmly yoked together by international bimetallism), will change so as to correspond to the changes in prices brought about by a variety of causes independent of the quantity of the precious metals. Under such circumstances, the attention given to the question of a proper standard of deferred payments can never be too careful.

BIBLIOGRAPHY.

BARBOUR (D.). The Theory of Bimetallism and the Effects of the Partial Demonetization of Silver on England and India. London: Cassell & Co. 1885.

BOURNE (S.). On Some Phases of the Silver Question. *Journal of the Stat. Soc.*, June, 1879.

FORSELL (H.). The Appreciation of Gold and the Fall in Prices of Commodities. London : Effingham Wilson. 1886. [Transl. from the Swedish.]

FOXWELL (H. S.). Irregularity of Employment and Fluctuations of Prices. Edinburgh: Co-operative Printing Co. 1886.

FOWLER (W.). Appreciation of Gold. An Essay. London: Cassell & Co. 1886.

———. The Present Low Prices and their Causes. *Contemp. Rev.*, April, 1885.

FREWEN (M.). Gold Scarcity and the Depression of Trade. *Nineteenth Century*, Oct., 1885.

GIBBS (H. H.). The Bimetallic Standard of Value. *Fortn. Rev.*, Oct., 1886.

GIFFEN (R.). On the Fall of Prices of Commodities in Recent Years. *Journal of the Stat. Soc.*, March, 1879.

———. Prices of Exports from 1861-1877. *Ibid.*, 1879, p. 305.

———. Trade Depression and Low Prices. *Contemp. Rev.*, June, 1885.

GOSCHEN (G. J.). On the Probable Results of an Increase in the Purchasing Power of Gold. *Journal of the Institute of Bankers*, April, 1883.

HANSARD (L.). On the Prices of Some Commodities during the Decade 1874-1883. *Ibid.*, Dec., 1884.

HOARE (H.). The Appreciation of Gold and its Connection with the Depression of Trade. London: Edward Stanford. 1886.

HORTON (S. D.). Rise in the Value of Gold. Report on the International Monetary Conference of 1878. pp. 385-408.

JEVONS (W. S.). The Variation of Prices. *Journal of the Stat. Soc.*, June, 1865.

LAVELEYE (E. de). The Economic Crisis and its Causes. *Contemp. Rev.*, May, 1886.

LEROY-BEAULIEU (P.). La Baisse des Prix et la Crise Commerciale. *Revue des Deux Mondes*, May 15, 1886.

———. The Fall in the Price of Commodities: Its Cause and Effect. *Journal of the Stat. Soc.* [Transl. from *Economiste Français*, April 12 and 19, 1884.]

——— Les Variations des Prix depuis Soixante Ans. Écon. Français, Feb. 19, 26.

MULHALL (M. G.). Balance Sheet of the World for the Years 1870-1880. London: Edward Stanford. 2d ed. 1881.

———. History of Prices since the Year 1850. London: Longmans. 1885.

———. Prices and the Gold Supply. *Contemp. Rev.*, Aug., 1885.

NASSE (E.). Die Währungsfrage in Deutschland. *Preussische Jahrbücher*, March, 1885.

O'CONOR (J. E.). Prices and Wages in India, Government of India, Department of Finance and Commerce. Calcutta. 1886.

PATTERSON (R. H.). Is the Value of Money rising in England, and throughout the World? *Journal of the Stat. Soc.*, March, 1880.

PIRMEZ (E.). La Crise: Examen de la Situation Économique de la Belgique. Brussels. 1884.

RAUCHBERG (H.). Die Entwickelung des Clearing-verkehres, eine
vergleichende Statistische Studie.
*Bulletin de l'Institut International
de Statistique*, I., 1886.

SAUERBECK (A.). Prices of Commodities and the Precious Metals.
Journal of the Stat. Soc., Sept.,
1886.

SCHMIDT (H.). The Silver Question
in its Social Aspect. London:
Effingham Wilson. 1886.

SOETBEER (A.). Materialien zur Er-
läuterung und Beurtheilung der
wirtschaftlichen Edel-metallver-
hältnisse und der Währungsfrage.
Berlin: Puttkammer & Mühl-
brecht. 2d ed. 1886.

——. Graphische Darstellungen
in Bezug auf die Silberfrage.

Berlin: Puttkammer & Mühl-
brecht. 1886.

——. Zur Statistik der Edel-
metalle, 1876 bis 1880. *Jahrbücher
für National-Oek.* N. F., III., B.
1881.

UNSIGNED. Dearness of Gold.
Quart. Rev., Oct., 1886.

——. The Scarcity of Gold. *Edinburgh Rev.*, Jan., 1886.

——. Modern Trade and the
Means of Exchange. *Ibid.*, July,
1886.

——. The Silver Question plainly
and practically considered by a
Free Trader. Liverpool: Walms-
ley. 1886.

——. Third Report of the Royal
Commission on the Depression of
Trade and Industry. *Parl. Doc.*,
1886.

APPENDIX.

I.

PRICES IN GREAT BRITAIN.

A.

PRICES PUBLISHED BY THE LONDON "ECONOMIST," S. BOURNE, AND R. H. I. PALGRAVE.

The first use of index numbers to represent the changes of prices was made by the late Mr. Newmarch in a table published in the "Annual Commercial History and Review" of the London *Economist*. The table is intended to show the movement of prices, during a series of years, for twenty-two articles in the English wholesale markets. Taking the average price for 1845–50, in every case, as the standard, represented by one hundred, the ratio of the price on January 1 and July 1 of every year is compared with this, the result being, in fact, a percentage. The sum of these percentages for twenty-two articles is the index number for the year, as twenty-two hundred is the index number for 1845–50. Division by twenty-two reduces the series of index numbers to average percentages. The articles selected are as follows:—

Coffee, sugar, tea, tobacco, wheat, butcher's meat, Surat cotton, raw silk, flax and hemp, wool, indigo, oils, timber, tallow, leather, copper, iron, lead, tin, Pernambuco cotton, cotton yarn, cotton cloth.

While probably the best known of all tables, the figures of the *Economist* are open to serious objections: (1) As the editors announce, the table "does not, of course, present a full and accurate representation of the variations of prices, inasmuch as it cannot allow for the relative importance of the different articles." Wheat, for example, counts for no more than indigo. (2) The quotations on a given day do not show the state of prices for the year. (3) The articles selected are too few in number to insure a proper view of prices in general. (4) The commodities are injudiciously chosen. There are four articles of cotton, causing serious distortion in the years 1862–67, and a disproportionate number of so-called raw materials. The continuity of the *Economist* table since 1850 (interrupted only for the years 1852, 1854–56) explains the importance ascribed to it.

In the *Journal of the Statistical Society* (June, 1879, pp. 413–417), Mr. Bourne corrected the figures of the *Economist* by using only one quotation of cotton goods instead of four (the average of the four) and by adding coal. His table contains the prices of only twenty articles, and ends with 1879, but, in other respects, is like that of the *Economist*.

Mr. Bourne also constructed a table from the prices of articles in the country of their production, using the average prices of the years 1872–77 as the basis for comparison. His figures are taken from "the average of the years' transactions shown in the *Statistical Abstracts for Foreign Countries and for Colonial Possessions*, issued from the Board of Trade," and run from 1860 to 1879, but for only seven articles,— wheat, cotton, wine, silk, rice, opium, and tea.

In order to get a comparison with some Indian prices, which date back only to 1865, Mr. R. H. Inglis Palgrave, in the Appendix to the *Third Report of the Royal Commission on Depression of Trade and Industry*, 1886, p. 330, rearranged the figures of the *Economist* by taking the prices of the years 1865–69, instead of the years 1845–50, as the basis for comparison.

Realizing the insufficiency of the method adopted in constructing the *Economist* table, Mr. Palgrave prepared another table, based on the prices of 1865–69, "in which allowance is made for the 'relative importance' of each of the articles selected, which are the same as those taken in the *Economist*." The relative importance of an article is reached by finding the relative proportions of the home trade in it (taking into account both quantities and values) to the total home trade in the twenty-two commodities. For example, in the year 1873, the home trade in cotton (raw) was £48,000,000, and in indigo £800,000, out of £306,450,000 for all the twenty-two articles. So cotton is assigned an importance of three hundred and forty-six, and indigo of only six, out of twenty-two hundred, the standard index number. Of course, both his tables are open to the same objections as that of the *Economist*, except in the matter of "relative importance."

| | Economist Table. | | | Bourne's Table. | | Palgrave's Tables. | | | |
| | | | | Basis of 1872-77. | | Economist on basis of 1865-69. | | Preceding corrected for relative importance. | |
	Index Numbers.	Reduced to Per cent.	Corrected by Bourne.	Home Prices.	World Prices.	Index Numbers.	Per cent.	Index Numbers.	Per cent.
1845–50	2200	100							
1851 Jan. 1	2293	104	103						
1853 July 1	2451	111	114						
1857 "	2996	136	140						
1858 Jan. 1	2612	118	123						
1859 "	2543	115	118						
1860 "	2692	122	123	94					
1861 "	2727	123	124	94	113				
1862 "	2878	130	125	95	116				
1863 "	3492	158	144	109	143				
1864 "	3787	172	151	115	170				
1865 "	3575	162	138	105	175			2366	108
1866 "	3564	161	141	107	132			2434	111
1867 "	3024	137	128	98	120	2200	100	2179	99
1868 "	2682	122	122	93	116			2058	93
1869 "	2666	121	118	90	111			1963	89
1870 "	2689	122	119	91	111	1995	91	1975	90
1871 "	2590	118	118	90	105	1981	90	2046	93
1872 "	2835	129	133 125	101	108	2132	97	2197	100
1873 "	2947	134	142 132	108	107	2237	102	2298	104
1874 "	2891	131	136 127	103	99	2207	100	2378	108
1875 "	2778	126	130 124	99	94	2098	95	2125	97
1876 "	2711	123	123	94	95	2044	93	2186	99
1877 "	2723	124	126	96	97	2004	94	2205	100
1878 "	2529	115	118	90		1910	87	2081	95
1879 "	2202	100	106	80		1676	76	1806	82
1880 "	2538	115				1918	87	1967	89
1881 "	2376	108				1782	81	2054	93
1882 "	2435	111				1830	83	1908	87
1883 "	2342	107				1755	80	1924	88
" July 1	2220	101							
1884 Jan. 1	2221	101				1660	75	1750	80
" July 1	2170	98							
1885 Jan. 1	2098	95				1562	70	1669	76
" July 1	2048	93							
1886 Jan. 1	2023	92				1509	69		

TABLE B.

PRICES COMPILED BY W. S. JEVONS.

In 1863, Professor W. Stanley Jevons published a pamphlet entitled *A Serious Fall in the Value of Gold ascertained, and its Social Effects set forth.* This was followed in 1865 by a paper in the *Journal of the Statistical Society,* vol. xxviii., pp. 294–320, on "The Variation of Prices and the Value of the Currency since 1782"; and, in 1869, by a letter to the *Economist,* vol. xxvii., pp. 530–532, on "The Depreciation of Gold." The three papers are reprinted in his collected *Investigations in Currency and Finance* (London, 1884).

In his first pamphlet, Jevons collated from various sources, chiefly from the *Economist*, the prices of thirty-nine articles, namely: —

I., silver, tin, copper, lead, bar iron, pig iron, tin plates; II., palm oil, linseed oil, tallow, hides, leather, timber, logwood, indigo; III., cotton (three grades), wool, silk, flax, hemp; IV., wheat, barley, oats, rye, beans, peas; V., hay, clover, straw, beef, mutton, pork, butter; VI., sugar, spirits, tea, pepper.

These prices were reduced in the following manner. The average of the monthly prices during each year was calculated,— apparently, the arithmetical mean was taken, though this is not stated. From the yearly prices thus obtained, the simple arithmetical average price of each commodity for the six years, 1845–50, was first drawn; and, with this six years' average as a base, the average price of every commodity for every year from 1845 to 1862 was compared. The results were expressed in percentages, the average of every commodity for 1845–50 being expressed by one hundred. When, however, the percentages of the thirty-nine commodities were averaged for any one year, in order to secure the final indicator of the state of general prices for that year, Jevons calculated the geometrical mean of the percentages. Substantially the same method was followed in the paper of 1865 in the *Statistical Journal*; but, in this case, the final result was indicated only by a diagram, no tables being given of general prices. The method was again used in the *Economist* letter of 1869; and this time a table was given, indicating for selected years before 1847, and for all years between 1847 and 1869, the course of average prices of "about fifty of the chief articles of commerce," which, however, are not further specified. As to the uses of the arithmetical or geometrical mean, see a note in this *Journal*, *ante*, pp. 83–86.

Column one gives Jevons's figures of general prices as calculated in the *Serious Fall*. Column two gives the figures of the *Economist* letter, in which the average for 1849 is taken as one hundred.

Years.	1. Average of 1845–50 taken as 100.	2. Average of 1849 taken as 100.	Years.	1. Average of 1845–50 taken as 100.	2. Average of 1849 taken as 100.
1789		133	1855	117.6	125
1799		202	1856	122.5	129
1809		245	1857	128.8	132
1819		175	1858	114.2	118
1829		124	1859	116.0	120
1839		144	1860	117.9	124
1845	104.4 ⎫		1861	115.1	123
1846	105.4 ⎪		1862	113.4	124
1847	110.8 ⎬ 100	122	1863		123
1848	94.1 ⎪	106	1864		122
1849	89.6 ⎭	100	1865		121
1850	92.1	101	1866		128
1851	92.4	103	1867		118
1852	93.8	101	1868		120
1853	111.3	116	1869		119
1854	120.7	130			

TABLE C.

PRICES COMPILED BY A. ELLIS.

In the London *Statist* of June 8, 1878, Mr. Arthur Ellis published a table of the prices of twenty-five articles, taking his quotations and quantities from the Board of Trade returns for imports. The prices of the year 1869 were taken as a standard for comparison; but the years compared are only 1859, 1873, 1876, and the first quarter of 1878. Mr. Ellis used certain index numbers to indicate the relative importance of commodities,— *e.g.*, cotton is rated at nineteen and indigo at one. The number 1000 multiplied by the index yields the standard for 1869, with which other years are compared. By this means, "the purchasing power of money can be arrived at in the various periods."

Articles imported or produced.	Index Numbers.	RELATIVE COST IN				
		1859.	1869 Stan'd.	1873.	1876.	First Quarter 1878.
Animals, oxen . . .	8	6,300	8,000	7,700	9,670	9,115
Animals, sheep	6	6,200	6,000	7,470	7,460	8,020
Butter	2	1,850	2,000	2,050	2,200	2,170
Cheese	1	810	1,000	950	880	1,110
Coffee . .	1	1,110	1,000	1,430	1,540	1,500
Wheat	15	13,270	15,000	18,750	15,030	17,655
Barley	3	2,630	3,000	3,100	2,200	3,230
Maize	2	1,990	2,000	2,050	1,900	2,000
Flour	4	4,110	4,000	5,370	4,570	5,200
Spirits	1	1,020	1,000	1,230	1,020	1,005
Sugar	4	4,230	4,000	3,900	3,410	3,640
Tea	3	3,120	3,000	2,840	2,840	2,635
Tobacco	1	910	1,000	910	1,000	945
Wine	2	2,230	2,000	2,480	2,290	2,325
Cotton	19	11,620	19,000	14,660	11,010	10,540
Indigo	1	820	1,000	760	650	655
Flax	3	2,930	3,000	2,650	2,660	3,130
Hides	1	1,070	1,000	1,190	1,240	910
Coal	8	7,720	8,000	17,430	9,060	8,065
Copper	1	1,530	1,000	1,250	1,140	1,010
Iron, raw	2	1,980	2,000	4,300	2,160	1,855
Silk	2	1,670	2,000	1,720	1,570	1,475
Tallow	1	1,220	1,000	900	940	880
Wood	2	2,240	2,000	2,480	2,190	2,160
Wool	7	9,090	7,000	7,490	7,980	7,245
	100	91,570	100,000	115,060	96,610	98,475

TABLE D.

PRICES COMPILED BY MR. GIFFEN.

In a Report to the English Board of Trade in 1885 on the Prices of Imports and Exports from 1861 to 1877, Mr. Robert Giffen presented a table of prices for exports in the period from 1840 to 1883, and for imports from 1854 to 1883. The table includes thirty-five articles, with index numbers in which the relative importance of the articles is expressed. "To get the 'index number,' my plan has been to ascertain the percentage proportions of the value of the exports of each enumerated article to the value of the whole export trade, in alternate years since 1861." (*Journal of Statistical Society*, 1879, pp. 66–68, 305–321.) Having ascertained the proportion of the value of the exports of each article to the whole export trade, he adds together the numbers thus obtained for the thirty-five articles. In this way, he obtains an initial index number, which he fixes upon as 65.8 for exports. In a similar way, he settles upon 81.16 for imports. "An index number being thus formed, an average rise or fall may be shown by calculating the percentage of the rise or fall of each article on the portion of the index number assigned to it, the differences between the percentages of increase or decrease constituting an addition to or a reduction from the index number, which immediately shows whether there has been an average rise or fall and how much." See also *Contemporary Review*, June, 1885, p. 812, for later figures. In the appendix to the *Third Report of the Royal Commission on the Depression of Trade and Industry*, p. 329, Mr. Palgrave gives Mr. Giffen's figures, rearranging them on a basis of one hundred, starting with 1840 for exports and with 1854 for imports, as follows:—

Year.	Exports. Base line of 1840.	Per Cent.	Exports. Base line of 1854.	Per Cent.	Imports. Base line of 1854.	Per Cent.
1840	79.14	100				
1841	76.75	97				
1845	71.85	91				
1848	63.37	80				
1849	60.51	76				
1852	59.33	75				
1853	64.66	82				
1854	64.85	82	64.85	100	80.36	100
1855	63.05	80	63.05	97	84.67	105
1857	66.57	84	66.57	103	88.24	110
1859	66.20	83	66.20	102	79.77	99
1865	89.26	112	89.26	137	94.75	118
1868	77.22	97	77.22	119	86.89	108
1873	85.73	108	85.73	132	85.59	107
1875	74.47	94	74.47	114	81.41	101
1876	68.05	86	68.05	105	77.55	96
1877	65.40	82	65.40	101	79.68	99
1878	.....	...	.....	...	74.12	92
1879	59.70	75	59.70	92	70.86	88
1880	.....	...	.....	...	74.77	93
1881	59.54	75	59.54	92	74.17	92
1883	59.85	76	59.85	92	71.73	89

TABLE E.

PRICES OF LEADING WHOLESALE COMMODITIES IN JANUARY. PREPARED BY MR. GIFFEN, "JOURNAL OF STATISTICAL SOCIETY," 1879, P. 61, AND CONTEMPORARY REVIEW, JUNE, 1885.

		Jan. 1873	1874	1875	1876	1877	1878	1879	1883	1885
Iron, Scotch pig,	ton	127s	107s 6d	80s	64s 3d	57s 6d	51s 6d	43s	47s 8d	41s 9d
Coal, Hetton, } " Wallsend, }	"	30s	27s 6d	30s	25s	19s	18s 6d	19s	17s 6d	18s
Copper, Chili bars,	"	£91	£84	£83 10s	£82	£75 10s	£66	£57	£65	£48½
Tin, Straits,	"	£142	£120	£94	£82	£75 10s	£66	£61	£93	£77½
Wheat, Gazette av.	qr.	55s 11d	62s 1d	44s 8d	45s 9d	51s 6d	51s 9d	39s 7d	40s 4d	34s 11d
" Red Spring, at New York,	bu.	$1.70	$1.69	$1.22	$1.33	$1.45	$1.45	$1.10	$1.18	$0.91
Flour, town made,	sack	47s 6d	53s 6d	38s 6d	42s 6d	40s	46s	37s	38s	32s
" New York,	bbl.	$7.50	$7.10	$5.15	$5.50	$6.00	$5.50	$3.70	$4.30	$3.25
Beef, inferior, } by carcass }	8 lbs.	3s 10d	3s 9d	3s 8d	4s 3d	3s 3d	2s 10d	2s 10d	4s 4d	4s
" prime small,	"	5s 3d	5s 5d	5s 5d	5s 3d	5s 2d	5s	4s 9d	6s	5s 4d
Cotton, Mid Upland,	lb.	10d	8½d	7½d	7d	6½d	6½d	5¾d	5¼d	6d
Wool,	pck.	£23	£19 15s	£18 5s	£17 10s	£16 10s	£15 10s	£13	£12	£11
Sugar, Manilla, } " Muscov., }	cwt.	21s 6d	18s	17s	15s	22s	14s 6d	16s	16s 6d	10s
Coffee, Ceylon, good, } ordinary, }	"	80s	112s 6d	84s	90s 6d	87s 6d	84s 9d	65s	78s 6d	71s
Pepper, blk. Malabar,	lb.	7d	8½d	7d	5¾d	5¾d	4½d	4½d	5¾d	8d
Saltpetre, foreign,	cwt.	29s	23s 9d	22s 6d	18s 6d	20s	22s	19s	19s	15s 3d

TABLE F.

PRICES COMPILED BY A. SAUERBECK.

In the *Journal of the Statistical Society* for September, 1886, Mr. Augustus Sauerbeck has presented a table of prices of thirty-eight articles for the period from 1846 to 1885, representing the average prices of the eleven years, 1867 to 1877, by one hundred. His index numbers are computed by taking the arithmetical mean of the quotations. "With but few exceptions," he says, "the prices given are the average prices in each year, either those officially returned or the averages of the twelve quotations at the end of each month, partly received from private firms, partly collected from the *Economist* and other publications. Where a range of prices is given, the mean has been taken between the highest and lowest quotations." The articles selected are as follows: —

I., wheat (two grades), flour, barley, oats, maize, potatoes, rice; II., beef (two grades), mutton (two grades), pork, bacon, butter; III., sugar (two grades), coffee, tea; IV., pig iron, bar iron, copper, tin, lead, coals (two grades); V., cotton (two grades), flax, hemp, jute, wool (two grades), silk; VI., hides, leather, tallow, palm oil, olive oil, linseed oil, petroleum (since 1872), soda crystals, nitrate of soda, indigo, timber.

(1) It is to be regretted that all the prices are not averages. (2) The relative importance of articles, also, is insufficiently represented; *e.g.*, olive oil has as great an influence on the index number as iron. (3) No satisfactory statement is made as to the sources from which he gets his quotations. (4) He admits that "it was impossible to retain exactly the same standard for this long period [1846 to 1885], owing to the frequent alterations of descriptions; and the old quotations for a few articles, such as sugar, coffee, and flax, must be considered as only approximately showing the course of prices." (5) The commodities are almost entirely raw produce. So that in sources of information, reliability, numbers of articles, and continuity of quotations on the same system, the most considerable collection of English prices falls behind the Hamburg table.

Year.	Vegetable Food (Corn, &c.)	Animal Food (Meat, &c.)	Sugar, Coffee, and Tea.	Total Food.	Minerals.	Textiles.	Sundry Materials.	Materials.	Grand Total.
1846	106	81	98	95	92	77	86	85	**89**
1847	129	88	87	105	94	78	86	86	**95**
1848	92	83	69	84	78	64	77	73	**78**
1849	79	71	77	76	77	67	75	73	**74**
1850	74	67	87	75	77	78	80	78	**77**
1851	73	68	84	74	75	75	79	76	**75**
1852	80	69	75	75	80	78	84	81	**78**
1853	109	82	87	91	105	87	101	97	**95**
1854	120	87	85	101	115	88	109	104	**102**
1855	120	87	89	101	109	84	109	101	**101**
1856	109	88	97	99	110	89	109	102	**101**
1857	105	89	119	102	108	92	119	107	**105**
1858	87	83	97	88	96	84	102	94	**91**
1859	85	85	102	89	98	88	107	98	**94**
1860	99	91	107	98	97	90	111	100	**99**
1861	102	91	96	97	91	92	109	99	**98**
1862	98	86	98	94	91	123	106	107	**101**
1863	87	85	99	89	93	149	101	115	**103**
1864	79	89	106	88	96	162	98	119	**105**
1865	84	97	97	91	91	134	97	108	**101**
1866	95	96	94	95	91	130	99	107	**102**
1867	115	89	94	101	87	110	100	100	**100**
1868	113	88	96	100	85	106	102	99	**99**
1869	91	96	98	94	89	109	100	100	**98**
1870	88	98	95	93	89	106	99	99	**96**
1871	94	100	100	98	93	103	105	101	**100**
1872	101	101	104	102	127	114	108	115	**109**
1873	106	109	106	107	141	103	106	114	**111**
1874	105	103	105	104	116	92	96	100	**102**
1875	93	108	100	100	101	88	92	93	**96**
1876	92	108	98	99	90	85	95	91	**95**
1877	100	101	103	101	84	85	94	89	**94**
1878	95	101	90	96	74	78	88	81	**87**
1879	87	94	87	90	73	74	85	78	**83**
1880	89	101	88	94	79	81	89	84	**88**
1881	84	101	84	91	77	77	86	89	**85**
1882	84	104	76	89	79	73	85	80	**84**
1883	82	103	77	89	76	70	84	77	**82**
1884	71	97	63	79	68	68	81	73	**76**
1885	68	88	63	74	66	65	76	79	**72**

TABLE G.

PRICES COMPILED BY M. G. MULHALL.

In his *History of Prices since the Year* 1850, Mr. Mulhall boldly sets his face against the use of index numbers for prices, and favors a "trade-level" method, which compares "the actual total of trade with the sums which the same volume of merchandise would have amounted to at previous periods, according to the prices then ruling" (p. 1, cf. also pp. 7, 79, 153–154). Giving little or no information as to his sources, his results must necessarily be distrusted. He uses, for instance, the unsatisfactory tables of Mr. Burchard for American prices as if they were unimpeachable. Taking the price level of 1841–50 as 100, his results to 1884 are as follows (based on the Board of Trade returns for imports and exports) : —

1854	103	1871	110
1855	104	1872	116
1856	105	1873	121
1857	111	1874	115
1858	103	1875	109
1859	104	Average	114
1860	107	1876	102
Average	105	1877	103
1861	107	1878	96
1862	114	1879	92
1863	133	1880	96
1864	152	Average	97
1865	138	1881	94
Average	129	1882	94
1866	139	1883	91
1867	126	1884	87
1868	121	Average	91¼
1869	121	1861–70	126
1870	110	1871–80	106
Average	123	1854–84	110

II.

PRICES IN GERMANY.

TABLE H.

PRICES COMPILED BY E. LASPEYRES.

In 1864, Professor E. Laspeyres made an investigation of Hamburg prices from 1831 to 1863, the results of which were published in the *Jahrbücher für National-Oekonomie*, vol iii. (old series), pp. 81–118, 209–236. His tables include forty-eight articles, of which the prices were ascertained for the first Friday of each month from the Hamburg *Allgemeiner Preiscourant*. The arithmetical mean of these monthly prices yielded the average for the year. The general average for the decade 1831 to 1840 was taken to be one hundred. His final figures were: —

Periods.		Average Prices.	Periods.		Average Prices.
Decade	1831-40	100	Year	1857	137.8
"	1841-50	95.4	"	1858	118.6
Year	1851	93.1	"	1859	119.2
"	1852	94.3	"	1860	125.4
"	1853	112.9	"	1861	125.7
"	1854	125.8	"	1862	125.4
"	1855	132.2	"	1863	122.2
"	1856	134.2	Decade	1854-63	126.4

TABLE J.

PRICES COMPILED BY H. PAASCHE AND R. VON DER BORGHT.

In 1874 and in 1882, two notes on prices were printed in the *Jahrbücher für National-Oekonomie*, vol. xxiii., pp. 171-173, and vol. xxxix. (vol. v. of new series), pp. 177-185. The first was signed by H. P. (H. Paasche) and the second by R. v. d. B. (R. v. d. Borght). The second was a continuation of the first, considering the same articles and using the same method. The method was an attempt to apply a coefficient to the price of different articles, according to their relative importance. Twenty-two articles were selected, and the quantity consumed of each in Germany in 1868 was ascertained as closely as possible. The price of each article was multiplied for each year by the consumption of 1868; and the sum of money which would buy the quantity consumed in 1868 of the whole twenty-two, or of any limited group, was then arrived at by addition. The totals were then arranged on a scale in which one hundred represented the average of the twenty years, 1847 to 1867. The twenty-year average or base was presumably ascertained by the same method, though it is not expressly so stated.

The twenty-two articles were arranged in six groups, as follows: —

I., coffee, cocoa, tea, pepper, rice, sugar; II., cotton, silk; III., indigo, saltpetre, fish-oil, palm oil; IV., pig iron, zinc, tin, copper, lead; V., coal; VI., wheat, rye, barley, oats.

To the final figures are appended, for comparison, those averages which would have resulted from a simple arithmetical mean taken irrespective of quantity.

Year.	General Average.	Average irrespective of quantity	Years.	General Average.	Average irrespective of quantity
1847-67	100	100	1875	103.2	106
1868	118.5	104	1876	102.9	106
1869	107.7	106	1877	104.1	105
1870	98	103	1878	92.1	96
1871	108	109	1879	90.3	98
1872	116.6	121	1880	96.9	87
1873	120.1	124			
1874	114.1	113	**1868-80**	**105.8**	**106**

TABLE K.

PRICES PUBLISHED BY A. SOETBEER.

In Dr. Soetbeer's *Materialien* (2d ed., 1886), pp. 99–114, are published the annual average prices, from 1847 to 1885, of each one of one hundred and fourteen articles, one hundred of which were computed by the officials of the *Handelsstatisches Bureau* at Hamburg, the prices of the fourteen remaining articles being taken from the British Board of Trade returns for exports. The Hamburg figures, with averages for five year periods, to 1880, were published by Dr. Soetbeer in 1881 in the *Jahrbücher für National-Oekonomie* (N. F., III., B). The index number of one hundred represents the mean of the average prices for the years 1847 to 1850. The average prices for each year and the number indicating the percentage which the price bears to the index number (1847 to 1850) are given for each article, for each of the eight groups, and for the total of the one hundred and fourteen articles. The method used is evidently the simple arithmetical mean : the relative importance of commodities is not considered.

Dr. Soetbeer points out that systematic official records are kept at Hamburg according to actual declarations of values and quantities, under many checks to insure accuracy. Since 1881, the Hamburg officials have carefully revised the whole table, so that it gives the most trustworthy wholesale prices of the largest number of articles since 1850 at present known to us.

The articles used in the Hamburg tables are : I., wheat, flour, rye, ryemeal, oats, barley, malt, buckwheat, peas, white beans, potatoes, hops, cloverseed, rape-seed, rape-seed oil, linseed oil, oil-cake, raw sugar, refined sugar, spirits ; II., beef, veal, mutton, pork, milk, butter, cheese, tallow, lard, hides, calf-skins, leather, horse-hair, bristles, bed-feathers, bones, buffalo-horns, glue, eggs, herring, dried fish, train-oil ; III., raisins, currants, almonds, dried prunes, olive oil, wine (French), champagne ; IV., coffee, cocoa, tea, pepper, allspice, cassia-bark, rice, sago, arrack, rum, tobacco, indigo, cochineal, logwood, rosewood, mahogany, rattan, palm oil, ivory ; V., coal, iron ore, bar iron, steel, lead, zinc, tin, copper, quicksilver, sulphur, saltpetre (Chili), salt, lime, cement ; VI., cotton, wool, flax, hemp, silk, cordage, rags ; VII., guano, gum elastic, gutta-percha, resin, pearl ash, pitch, potash, soda, stearine candles, tar, wax ; VIII., cotton yarn, plain piece-goods, printed cotton piece-goods, cotton stockings and socks, sewing thread, common glass bottles, linen yarn, plain linen, sail-cloth, woollen and worsted yarn, woollen cloth, flannels, worsteds, carpets.

Year.	I. Agricultural.	II. Animal	III. Tropical, &c.	IV. East India Goods, &c.	V. Mineral.	VI. Textile Materials.	VII. Divers.	VIII. British Exports.	(I–VIII.) Total of 114 articles.
1847–1850	100.00	100.00	100.00	100.00	100.00	100.00	100.00	100.00	**100.00**
1851	99.02	110.38	90.00	99.94	95.70	104.39	103.98	97.98	**100.21**
1852	110.71	106.68	95.33	99.95	95.76	105.01	95.09	95.98	**101.69**
1853	128.18	114.94	124.78	115.28	109.24	101.43	105.17	100.61	**113.69**
1854	150.49	121.12	112.91	118.17	115.95	111.64	119.44	99.53	**121.25**
1855	158.82	123.54	142.03	121.02	119.10	103.58	109.63	98.27	**124.23**
1851–1855	129.99	114.79	110.43	110.97	107.03	105.20	106.65	98.47	**112.22**
1856	149.03	127.61	155.95	123.95	116.65	100.02	100.50	98.50	**123.27**
1857	138.11	140.18	169.32	140.32	124.58	112.18	108.01	101.25	**130.11**
1858	119.92	127.02	120.69	112.76	109.04	103.59	99.70	100.91	**113.52**
1859	119.48	130.69	113.40	115.74	108.57	104.69	115.57	105.77	**116.34**
1860	133.75	133.75	120.36	120.28	108.66	108.74	116.83	105.60	**120.98**
1856–1860	131.84	132.31	134.72	122.61	113.59	107.12	108.21	102.41	**120.91**
1861	131.46	124.79	122.08	117.19	102.40	110.85	119.65	105.84	**118.10**
1862	126.80	127.19	113.93	117.28	101.88	124.31	156.99	114.22	**122.65**
1863	120.12	124.12	114.97	116.87	102.92	151.84	161.36	133.45	**125.49**
1864	117.89	129.21	109.41	125.74	104.53	154.26	162.58	146.53	**129.28**
1865	126.48	135.23	114.01	116.11	98.93	117.80	121.06	137.80	**122.63**
1861–1865	124.46	128 24	114.13	118.64	102.11	131.83	144.33	127.56	**123.59**
1866	137.64	135.64	126.30	117.90	96.64	134.94	111.30	140.36	**125.85**
1867	146.38	132.68	126.44	114.35	93.28	130.31	108.13	133.91	**124.44**
1868	141.59	133.48	120.75	116.75	91.76	127.18	101.25	127.56	**121.99**
1869	132.40	143.25	115.58	122.10	96.33	130.52	98.17	128.15	**123.38**
1870	131.23	139.32	118.57	120.56	99.68	122.87	111.21	122.68	**122.87**
1866–1870	137.74	136.35	121.54	118.32	95.47	129.17	105.90	130.55	**123.57**
1871	144.76	144.14	122.99	120.22	101.85	119.23	117.48	122.64	**127.03**
1872	144.17	155.82	125.36	130.25	121.63	122.79	128.54	130.07	**135.62**
1873	146.21	156.72	132.15	134.32	140.60	119.58	119.14	128.52	**138.28**
1874	150.99	157.76	145.02	136.74	116.70	112.80	112.21	126.06	**136.20**
1875	138.16	158.59	131.35	132.11	107.49	111.47	98.74	124.96	**129.85**
1871–1875	144.90	154.57	131.50	130.72	116.90	117.17	114.98	126.44	**133.29**
1876	141.06	155.79	128.69	129.74	106.27	105.54	101.78	119.23	**128.33**
1877	145.34	152.51	140.55	130.29	98.87	108.33	99.80	114.04	**127.70**
1878	132.50	141.53	134.34	125.61	94.14	102.33	97.24	111.03	**120.60**
1879	132.92	137.60	139.10	123.34	84.28	98.76	90.21	105.93	**117.10**
1880	138.11	147.30	154.65	122.92	88.33	96.72	95.23	108.15	**121.89**
1876–1880	138.12	146.76	138.91	126.38	94.35	102.33	96.79	111.70	**123.07**
1881	137.50	151.21	146.57	122.60	84.87	99.29	94.89	103.08	**121.07**
1882	138.45	155.17	139.23	122.47	86.99	95.10	99.10	104.72	**122.14**
1883	143.33	156.40	142.38	120.17	82.93	95.93	95.38	104.72	**122.24**
1884	123.85	150.26	120.16	117.90	78.69	97.02	84.82	103.36	**114.25**
1885	110.75	140.45	123.78	116.39	74.23	95.89	81.35	100.48	**108.72**
1881–1885	130.77	150.65	134.41	119.91	81.55	96.65	91.11	103.28	**117.68**

III.

PRICES IN FRANCE.

TABLE L.

PRICES COMPILED BY R. H. I. PALGRAVE.

In the *Third Report of the Royal Commission on the Depression of Trade and Industry*, Appendix, pp. 354–361, Mr. R. H. Inglis Palgrave has collected, from information given him by M. Léon Say and M. de Foville, and from the figures of the *Commission Permanente des Valeurs de Douane*, two tables of French prices for the period from

Year.	Table 28.	Table 28 reduced to scale of 100.	Table 29.	Table 29 reduced to scale of 100.
1865	2,267	103	2,331	106
1866	2,314	105	2,380	108
1867	2,207	100	2,144	97
1868	2,126	97	2,110	96
1869	2,087	95	2,045	93
	2,200	**100**	**2,200**	**100**
1870	2,137	97	2,000	91
1871	2,283	104	2,250	102
1872	2,434	111	2,310	105
1873	2,423	110	2,300	105
1874	2,223	101	2,125	97
1875	2,243	102	2,085	95
1876	2,196	100	2,090	95
1877	2,241	102	2,107	96
1878	1,950	89	2,010	91
1879	1,898	86	1,915	87
1880	1,941	88	1,937	88
1881	1,880	85	1,900	86
1882	1,845	84	1,855	84
1883	1,807	82	1,756	80
1884	1,679	76		

1865 to 1884 for twenty-two articles. The index number of twenty-two hundred (or one hundred) is taken to represent the average prices of the years 1865–69. The articles chosen and the method of computing the index numbers in Table 28 are as nearly as possible like those of the *Economist*. Table 29, however, introduces a method of ascertaining the relative importance of articles by finding the value of the actual imports into France of each commodity, as compared with the total value of the imports of all the twenty-two articles ; *e.g.*, in 1871, the importance of wheat was expressed by 330, and of butter by 6, out of the total 2200 ; but, in 1877, wheat was expressed by 166, and butter, 11. The final results of both methods are here given in parallel columns. In Table 28, the articles are : coffee, sugar, wheat, beef, butter, rice, tobacco, oil-seed, olive oil, tallow, raw silk, silk stuffs, gloves, raw cotton, raw wool, woollens, hides, coal, iron ore, copper ore, lead ore, and zinc.

IV.

PRICES IN THE UNITED STATES.

TABLE M.

PRICES COMPILED BY H. C. BURCHARD.

Mr. H. C. Burchard, in his report as Director of the Mint for 1881, gave the results of calculations of average prices in New York for the fifty-six years from 1825 to 1880. The figures are printed in the *Report on the Finances*, 1881, pp. 312–321. They are continued for the year 1881 in the *Report on the Finances*, 1882, pp. 252–254; for the year 1882 in *ibid.*, 1883, pp. 316–318; and for the years 1883 and 1884 in the *Report of the Director of the Mint on the Production of the Precious Metals*, 1884, pp. 499, 500. Mr. Burchard's first table, for the years 1825–80, is reprinted without change in the *Quarterly Reports of the Bureau of Statistics*, 1883–84, No. 3, pp. 328–387, and is agaiu reprinted, still without change, in the *Quarterly Reports*, etc., 1885–86, No. 3, pp. 556–565. Mr. Burchard wrote in 1881: "The prices quoted were obtained for the years 1825 to 1874, inclusive, from the tables of their average prices in New York, found in the *Finanre Reports* of 1863, 1873, and 1874. [See *Finance Report*, 1863, pp. 284–361; *ibid.*, 1873, pp. 502–541; *ibid.*, 1874, pp. 557–561.] For the succeeding six years, they were compiled in this office from the published semi-weekly quotations in the New York *Shipping and Commercial List*, from which paper, it is understood, the quotations were taken in compiling the tables found in the *Finance Reports.*" An examination of the *Finance Report* tables indicates that they were not compiled with great care. The price of an article will run along without change from month to month; then, suddenly, it will rise or fall sharply. The prices of articles that normally would fluctuate together (pig and bar iron, butter and cheese) show a very loose correspondence. Moreover, the same articles do not appear from year to year. An article will be quoted for a number of years, will then disappear, and later, perhaps, will reappear. Thus, flax does not appear till 1864, is quoted till 1878, and drops out thereafter. Again, Mr. Burchard's tables do not use all the *Finance Report* prices, but choose from among them. His averages, as finally given, are obtained from the prices of eighty-two articles in 1825, eighty-one in 1862, sixty-eight in 1864, sixty-five in 1880, and ninety iu 1884. Pork is quoted in ten forms for 1884, in only three forms in 1880; and it does not appear whether each form of pork was used as an independent factor in calculating the final result, or whether all were averaged in order to give one figure for pork. For the years 1862–78, the prices are reduced to a gold basis; but it is not indicated in what manner this reduction was effected.

Notwithstanding these serious imperfections, we reprint Mr. Burchard's figures for the years 1850–84, since they are the only continuous figures of average prices in the United States. They are the arithmetical means for each year of the prices of the varying number of commodities taken for that year. The index number 100 in the first column indicates the mean of all the prices for the fifty-six years, 1825–80: —

Year.	Basis of 1825–1850.	Reduced to basis of 1845–1850.	Year.	Basis of 1825–1850.	Reduced to basis of 1845–1850.
1850	88.9	102.6	1868	107.6	124.2
1851	89.3	103.1	1869	108.2	124.9
1852	91.9	106.1	1870	118.1	136.5
1853	99.4	114.8	1871	108.1	124.8
1854	107.0	123.5	1872	112.6	130.0
1855	111.1	128.3	1873	107.6	124.1
1856	112.2	129.6	1874	106.8	123.3
1857	119.8	138.3	1875	98.3	113.5
1858	99.7	115.1	1876	94.2	108.9
1859	100.6	116.1	1877	98.0	113.2
1860	100.3	115.8	1878	88.0	101.6
1861	98.0	113.1	1879	94.7	109.1
1862	111.6	128.8	1880	90.3	104.3
1863	119.4	137.8	1881	102.7	118.4
1864	110.1	127.0	1882	103.3	119.1
1865	123.0	142.0	1883	100.2	115.6
1866	119.1	137.5	1884	91.2	105.3
1867	113.0	130.5			

TABLE N.

PRICES COMPILED BY W. M. GROSVENOR.

Mr. W. M. Grosvenor published in the New York *Public* for January 19, 1882 (the journal not appearing since 1883), lists of prices of about fifty articles, covering the years from 1878 to 1882 as compared with 1860. His method is perhaps more valuable than his results. He estimates the quantity of each article consumed in the country *per capita* (see also *Public,* June 27, 1878), and multiplies that quantity by the price. The sum total of the results gives the amount of money necessary to buy the total consumption of the fifty articles in 1880.

The articles quoted are: —

I., wheat, corn, oats, barley, rye, beans, peas; II., pork, lard, beef, tallow, sheep; III., butter, cheese, milk, hay, eggs, rice, vegetables, fruit; IV., sugar, molasses, coffee, tea, tobacco, whiskey, beer, ale, fish, salt, spices; V., cotton, manufactures of cotton, wool, manufactures of wool, leather, manufactures of leather, silk, manufactures of silk, rubber, manufactures of rubber; VI., iron, manufactures of iron, coal, oil, tin, manufactures of tin, lead, manufactures of lead, copper, manufactures of copper, hemp, manufactures of hemp; VII., lumber, brick, lime, glass, paint, oil, turpentine, soap.

He does not, however, work out the *per capita* consumption for each year, but uses that of 1880 for all years. The discrepancies between the results given in different issues of the *Public* suggest a doubt as to the care with which the method was worked out in detail. We give the last and most complete table printed: —

Articles.	1860.			1878.	1879.	1880.	1881.		1882.
	Jan.	May.	Nov.	Nov.	Nov.	Nov.	Nov.	Dec.	Jan. 1.
Breadstuffs, . . .	$26.79	$26.71	$24.12	$18.02	$23.87	$21.86	$26.96	$26.57	$26.92
Meats, ...	11.50	12.12	11.37	9.67	10.19	11.50	12.94	12.63	13.34
Dairy and garden, .	13.92	13.01	11.91	9.94	12.28	12.74	16.94	18.26	16.68
Sugar, tea, etc., . .	8.69	8.70	9.19	11.91	12.73	12.26	12.94	12.72	12.10
All food, ...	60.90	60.54	56.59	49.54	59.07	58.36	69.83	70.18	69.04
Clothing, ...	31.12	31.72	32.11	27.70	31.96	31.01	31.43	31.74	31.63
Metals, ...	27.70	27.40	27.56	18.20	23.67	23.10	23.95	23.93	24.16
Lumber, glass, etc.,	15.12	15.60	15.43	13.33	14.01	16.18	15.79	15.86	15.92
Total, ...	$134.84	$135.26	$131.69	$108.77	$128.71	$128.65	$141.00	$141.71	$140.75
Equivalents, . .	$99.69	$100.00	$97.38	$80.41	$95.16	$95.11	$104.24	$104.77	$104.06

He also applied the quantitative method to some earlier years in comparison with 1860, the results of which are given herewith: —

Years.	Total.	Percentages.
1825	$1,942	108.5
1837	1,952	109.
1843	1,206	67.4
1860	1,790	**100.**
1877	2,067	115.
1878	1,624	90.7

9 7 8 3 7 4 4 7 3 9 5 9 7